SAY YES TO YOUR POTENTIAL

SAY **YES** TO YOUR POTENTIAL

SKIP ROSS
WITH CAROLE C. CARLSON

WORD PUBLISHING
Dallas · London · Sydney · Singapore

SAY "YES" TO YOUR POTENTIAL

Scripture quotations in this publication are from the following sources:
 The King James Version of the Bible (KJV).
 The New International Version of the Bible (NIV), published by the Zondervan Corporation, copyright © 1978 by the New York International Bible Society.
 The Living Bible, Paraphrased (TLB), copyright © 1971 by Tyndale House Publishers, Wheaton, Illinois.
 The New American Standard Bible (NASB), copyright 1960, 1962, 1963, 1968, 1971, 1972, 1975 by the Lockman Foundation.

An effort has been made to locate sources and obtain permission where necessary for the quotations used in this book. In the event of any unintentional omission, modifications will be gladly incorporated in future editions.

Library of Congress Cataloging in Publication Data

Ross, Skip.
 Say yes to your potential.

 Bibliography: p.
 1. Christian life—1960–   . 2. Success. 3. Ross, Skip. I. Carlson, Carole C. II. Title.
 BV4501.2.R668 1983   248.4   83–6995
 ISBN 0–8499–0309–2
 ISBN 0-8499 3014-6 (pbk.)

 98 RRD 9876543

With the gratitude of a father's heart, I dedicate this effort to my daughters, CINDY and KIM. Through the love of my heavenly Father, who has taught me, I give this teaching to them as the finest expression of my love. And to SUSAN, my wife, whose unquestioning love and devotion sustain me in this journey called LIFE.

CONTENTS

7

1

CLIMBING UP
FROM THE BOTTOM

The stage was bare, except for the man, the microphone, and his message. Several hundred people sat in the audience listening to the main attraction on the program: the featured motivational speaker. I was trying to pay attention, but I thought, *I've heard all this stuff before. What can he tell me that's new?* Then he made a remark that made my blood boil. I sat up straighter and felt a flush come into my face; in fact, I became so upset that I blocked out the remainder of his talk. The statement may seem innocuous, but it was earthshaking to me; it changed the direction of my life.

He said, "You have right now exactly what you want."

I wanted to shout, "That's not true!" but instead I tucked the frayed cuffs of my shirt up the sleeves of an out-of-style sport coat, I knew that my bank account couldn't handle new clothes, and I wanted to punch the smile off his face. What did he know about me? When I left that meeting I would return to a one-room apartment in North Hollywood, California, and stare at four drab walls. My personal life was a shambles, my business career collapsing. Although I had been raised in a Christian home and studied to become a minister, my spiritual life was wavering and dry.

On the outside I thought I was fooling the world. The facade I presented was that of a confident business leader with purpose and goals. But when I stripped off my mask and looked in the mirror I saw the real me: defeated, discouraged, depressed.

The reflection stared back, mocking and probing my thoughts: *How do you like what you see, Skip? Are you proud of what you've made of your life? What's happened to the boy who memorized the most Bible verses to win the baseball glove? Where did the guy go who was president of the student body at college? Where's the man who has preached and sung about God's greatness? What happened to your dream of being a recording artist or a top-notch communicator?*

I pounded my fist into my hand, disgusted with the answers I gave myself and haunted by the incessant voice that said, "You have right now exactly what you want."

Could that be an accurate statement? Was I, in fact, responsible for the kind of life I was leading? Maybe my circumstances were caused by my parents, my brother, friends, teachers, or business associates. It had to be somebody else's responsibility, didn't it? But I had to admit he was right; all my thoughts at that point in my life were centered on my failures and rejections. I worried about that all the time.

St. Bernard, a monk who lived almost nine hundred years ago, understood this truth: "Nothing can work me damage except myself. The harm that I sustain I carry about with me and I am never a real sufferer but by my own fault."

The result of that confrontation with the person I was, the man I didn't want to be, was the beginning of an intense life-changing search for the next eighteen months. My life was falling apart, and I had to learn to regulate the input which was destroying me. Some of my friends thought my process for regaining control was fanatical, because during that time I stopped reading newspapers and magazines. I turned off my radio and television set and avoided every negative conversation I could. Each day I spent three to five hours, sometimes much longer, reading inspirational books and listening to motivational tapes. Early in this process I rediscovered a Scripture I had learned in childhood: "As a man thinketh in his heart, so is he." It was a principle that became more convicting as the months passed. Whatever a person focuses his thoughts upon becomes reality in his life.

Seven days a week, for a year and a half I read the Scriptures and every positive piece of literature I could find. I went to lectures and listened to recordings of success-minded speakers. I would read or hear something that illuminated my thinking, and find the same principle verified in the Bible. Or a biblical truth would stir me, and I then discovered that it worked in practical everyday encounters.

If that sounds so obvious that it's almost simplistic, then you may not have grown up in a legalistic church background that gave you a list of do's and don'ts for every aspect of your life. I did. However, I did grow up to believe that the Bible is the inspired Word of God, and that is one of the reasons it was my most important study source.

There is a well-known psychiatrist in New York who doesn't believe in the Bible as the divinely inspired revelation of God. Still he prefaces treatment for depressed patients with this question: "Do you believe the Bible is the Word of God?" They either say, "yes" or "no." If they say "yes," he says, "Fine, here's a list of Scriptures. Take them home and read them two hours every morning and come back in a week to see me." If the answer is "no," he says, "Fine, here's a list of Scriptures: I want you to read them two hours every morning and two hours every afternoon." The only difference in the prescription is a double dose for the nonbeliever.

Whether you believe in the spiritual things of life or not, you will be able to apply the formula and principles in this book to your life, whoever you are and whatever your background. Your life can be changed, just as mine was.

The Price of Your Time

Right now you are exchanging something priceless to read this book. You are giving your time for this information. It must be worth it.

God gives us each day to use as we will. We can waste it or use it for good. When tomorrow comes this day will be gone forever, leaving something in its place we have traded for it. The day can be used for gain, not loss, for good, not evil, and for success, not failure.

We all have exactly the same amount of time to invest in making things happen. We can waste the time worrying about what might happen, or spend time fretting about what did happen. I firmly believe that the person who says, "I would do it if I could find the time," will not find time for anything. If we want time, we'll have to make it.

The measure of our accomplishment in life is not the measure of time that we have to do things, but it is a measure of what we do with the time that we have, with the talents that we have.

Right now, I am going to challenge you to *do* more than you have ever done before in your life with what you have. I'm going to challenge you to *be* more than you ever dreamed you could be and to do more than you thought you could do. I'm challenging you to become *all* you were created to be. I know it's possible.

I Dare You

I know that within each one of us is far more potential, more capacity than we may be able to envision. One of the most exciting aspects of my entire life is the knowledge that I can challenge people to be more than what they have believed they are, because I became more than what I was. The experiences of my own life will be used for illustration to let you know that if someone else has done it, you can, too. Some of you may have reached a quality of enviable success in your lives, others may feel like they're dragging through the "slough of despond." In *Pilgrim's Progress,* Christian had begun to sink in the mire of the swamp when a fellow came along (whose name, by the way, was Help) and said to poor Christian, "Hey, Buddy, what are you doing down there in the mud?" That's not exactly the way John Bunyan said it, but it's a modern version. Sometimes we are all in the position of wishing someone would come along and just pull us up from our circumstances.

Wherever you see yourself on the road of life, everything you have experienced on the journey has prepared you for this moment. Pascal once said: "Our achievements of today are but the sum total of our thoughts of yesterday. You are today where the thoughts of yesterday have brought you and you will be tomorrow where the thoughts of today take you."

For some of you the concepts you are about to read will be entirely new. You may compare me to the farmer who goes out for the first time to plow and till the soil that has never been plowed. Some of you may be ready for planting of the seed, so I will be as the farmer who is planting in that freshly cultivated soil. Some of you have already been plowed and planted, and you're ready for some cultivation; a little tender loving care, some words of encouragement may be what you need right now. The seeds someone else has planted may need irrigation, and a few weeds that have started may need pulling. However, there are others who are ripe for the harvest, because everything that has happened up to this particular point in your life has prepared you for the formula which follows.

Wherever you are in this growing process, there is one thing you can be sure of: you can be a different kind of person. In fact, you can be any kind of person that you choose to be.

Position Your Disposition

For years psychologists have tried to do studies on traits of optimism and negativism. Does heredity have anything to do with these qualities? Do circumstances govern the attitudes? I believe you are responsible for your own attitudes, and what I want to do is bring you face to face with yourself as a person and help you understand the greatness that dwells within you. *You are responsible for the kind of life you are living.*

There are positive people and there are negative people. You've probably known some of each. The negative person is always criticizing. He (or she) is looking for the reason why something won't work. The negative person is skeptical, frequently to the point of being cynical.

The positive person, on the other hand, is always open, he or she sees reasons why things will be successful and always looks at the good in people and in ideas.

Behavioral psychologists wanted to study the effect of environment on attitudes and chose two little boys of the same age and placed them in two rooms. The instructions were simple: "Go in and play for just an hour, and then we'll be back to check on you." Billy went into one room where every conceivable toy and game a boy would enjoy were displayed. There were trucks, soldiers, roller skates, video games, all chosen with his age and sex in mind. Johnny walked into the other room and found it filled with horse manure. After an hour or so the researchers went back to the rooms and opened the doors. They were astounded to see Billy sitting despondently in the middle of the floor, crying his heart out, surrounded by the lavish group of toys. "Why, Billy, what's the matter?" they asked.

"One of the wheels on the truck broke, I couldn't figure out how to work the games, and I hate roller skates This isn't any fun," he wailed. There was something wrong with every single toy in the room!

Then they went to the other room where Johnny was confined with the odious mess, opened the door and saw the gleeful boy just flinging the stuff around with joyful abandon. "Johnny, what are you doing?"

"I'm having a ball like you told me!"

"But in a room filled with horse manure, how can you?"

"Wow, this is exciting! I figured with all this stuff there has to be a pony in here someplace!"

After using that ludicrous illustration hundreds of times I experienced a similar circumstance. My wife, Susan, and I have a ranch in Rockford, Michigan, where we have a program to teach children the concepts of dynamic living contained in this book. Now I'm not a country boy, but we thought it would be a good idea for the camp kids to be involved in a farm experience. One day I came home and said, "I found a tractor I'd like to buy." Susan had a picture of one of those little machines you use to mow a lawn. However, the next day when I brought it home, she was astounded. The wheels on that contraption were taller than she was!

I had already bought all the cutting and baling equipment so I decided the time had come to use my new tractor. My first chore was to move a lot of loose straw near one barn over to the horse barn where we could use it for bedding the horses. As I maneuvered this giant closer to the barn where it would be easier to unload, I realized I had made a mistake. That big tractor began to sink! No one had told me that for seventy years that was the spot where they dumped the processed hay when the horses were done with it. Is that graphic enough?

It looked like good solid earth to my untrained eyes, but when those giant wheels began to sink in the soft gooey ground, I thought, *I'll just put it in low gear, give it the gas and go right on through.* Well, I went right on down, and the back wheels were flinging debris everyplace. That stuff was flying in the air like a Roman rocket that was set off on the ground. It hit everything, including my friend, who was standing behind the tractor. We were pelted from every direction. My friend, who had heard the negative and positive boy story many times, shouted at me, "Hey, Skip, if you think Johnny could fling that stuff, you ain't seen nothin' yet!"

The situation was so funny, and yet to a negative thinker it could have ruined the day.

Painful Change

As human beings we tend to seek the comfort of the familiar; therefore, change is always painful and we tend to resist it. Those eighteen months when I never watched television, listened to the radio, read a newspaper, or became involved in a negative conversation were very important in my life. When I've told others about that period in my life, they sometimes challenge the idea. One young girl who heard me speak found herself in a dilemma, much later, when she returned to school. She wrote me: "I have a challenge. We started school Wednesday and went through each of our subjects to meet all of our teachers. History was our last subject. The teacher told us that every day we had to either listen to the radio or read the newspaper to find news to discuss in class.

Since we are graded on it, I thought I could get news like, 'So and so tames a robin,' or something like that. But he said it must pertain to the world and it must be front page news. What shall I do? How shall I do it positively?''

Of course, she had to do her homework, but at least she recognized at a very young age that most news is negative. On the other hand, for a business person to refrain from reading the newspaper is a difficult decision. For me, the desired results were worth this denial.

I knew I had to be a different person. I knew my attitude needed adjustment, but I didn't know how to begin. I had goals, but had shoved them in the closet with my worn-out, tarnished dreams.

However, dreams can and do come true. Many of you have dreams, and you've buried them because someone came along and shot you down—not with a gun or a club, but with some simple words, "It can't be done." "Whatever makes you think you can do that?" "It won't work."

A friend of mine, Kitty Chappell of Ojai, California, wrote this poem:

ROBBED

The dangerous people are not the ones
. Who hit you with clubs and rob you with guns;
The thief won't attack your character traits
Or belittle your abilities to your face!
It likely will be a well-meaning friend
Who merely crushes your will to win.
No, he doesn't rob you, at point of gun,
He simply says, "It can't be done."
When pointed to thousands who already are
He smiles and says, "They're superior!
Personality-wise, and abilities, too,
They're way ahead of what others can do!"
It matters not that his words are untrue
For, you feel "others" *must* know *you!*
So, you're robbed of your hopes, your
        dreams to succeed.
Robbed of the material blessings received,
Robbed of your faith that says, "I can,"

And robbed by an ignorant, gunless friend.
So, the deadliest of men is not he with a gun,
But the one who tells you "It can't be done!"
For that taken by burglars can be gotten again.
But, what can replace your will to win?

Living the Dream

When I was a youngster, I used to dream about a time when I would speak before large audiences. However, I was very shy and would only speak when spoken to, smile when smiled at. In my fantasy, however, I would stand on a stage with some of the finest speakers in this country. One day, much later, after developing and sharing the Formula for Dynamic Living, I found myself standing before an audience of twelve thousand people, who had paid to hear me speak. They may have come to hear Paul Harvey, Norman Vincent Peale, Dr. Robert Schuller, Earl Nightingale, or Zig Ziglar, but I was also on the platform.

How could this be? What pulled this bashful, insecure, self-admitted failure up to sharing the platform with some of the best motivational speakers in the country? That's what this book is all about.

What is it you want to do? Are you achieving your dreams and goals? Will the formula that worked for me apply to your life?

Someone came to one of my Dynamic-Living Seminars and said, "I got so excited about what you said in the seminar that I went home flying on cloud nine for two weeks until I decided it wouldn't work, just like I thought."

Fortunately, she came to a second seminar, and her convictions lasted for months this time. She said, "I was so frustrated I could have wrung your neck." (I know the feeling.) However, she came to session three and four until finally she was able to grasp and begin to apply the principles.

The words you are about to read will profit you, not because I say so, not because they have changed my life, but because the formula and the principles are as true as the physical laws of our universe you accept and live with every day.

Begin today. I received a letter from my friend, Billy Zeoli, president of Gospel Films, that emphasizes the importance of immediate action. He wrote:

> Today is a treasure given to me in the same quantity of seconds, minutes, and hours that are given to other men.
>
> I am determined
>   not to waste time in worrying about what might happen,
>   but to invest my time in making things happen.
> I will not think
>   of what could be done if I were different.
>   I'm not different. I will do with what I have.
> I will not say, "If I could find the time. . . ."
>   because I will not *find* time for anything.
>   If I want time, I'll have to make it.
> I will begin by doing
>   and not wasting the precious time I have.
> I will seek to improve myself
>   because I will be needed and
>   I must not be found wanting.
>
> Doing the necessary, avoiding the unnecessary, I will
>   live today fully—as though it were my last day on earth.
> Don't expect to find me waiting for tomorrow—
>   It never comes.

The Magic Formula for Dynamic Living is impartial and without prejudice. It applies to young and old, educated and unschooled, wealthy and poor. It can be applied in all areas of your life. The only prerequisite is your desire to learn and your willingness to believe and apply.

This formula is not an invention, it is a discovery. When some of the treasures have been revealed, more are underneath, just waiting to surface. Your dreams can become reality, and you can become all you were created to be.

2

THE MAGIC FORMULA

The pastor of a small church decided that one of the ways he could attract business people in the community into his congregation was to hold a positive-thinking seminar and invite local merchants and professionals to attend. He wanted Merrill Womach, who was president of the record company for which I recorded, but he was busy. I was sent in as the substitute performer, a fact that concerned the pastor considerably.

When the time for the program arrived, the pastor was excited because over four hundred people had crowded into the rented auditorium—and his total congregation was only about one hundred.

My opening remarks for the Positive-Thinking Seminar were: "Positive thinking does not always work." It got everyone's attention, especially the pastor who had invited me as guest speaker. In fact, I thought the poor fellow would faint.

It is true, though, that positive thinking does not always work—particularly when it is in direct contrast to the person you believe yourself to be. Some people read books, listen to tapes and go to seminars on positive thinking and know that the glow of what they have read or heard lasts until the first rejection, the next disappointment, or last phone call. Sure, positive thinking helps, but

it's not always the complete answer. The concept of positive thinking can sometimes be compared to taking medicine for temporary
relief, without treating the source of the illness.

The Formula Was Born

Almost two years after my resolve to study and eliminate the
negative drains from my life, a business associate of mine said,
"Skip, something's happened to you. You're different. Tell me
about it." I tried to explain to him the process of change that I had
undergone, and he asked me to share these concepts with a few
others. Soon I was speaking to larger and larger meetings, and
eventually the Dynamic-Living Seminars were born.

One night I heard a speech by Rich DeVos, the president of the
Amway Corporation, and he used a formula which was:

$MMW = (NR + HE) \times T$ (Man's Material Welfare equals
Natural Resources plus Human Energy times Tools.)

Wow! It was something one could remember when explaining
the free enterprise system. Why couldn't I develop a formula that
could be memorized and cause total recall to what I said? I did, and
here is the magic formula:

$$DL = (GGE + PS) \times PSI$$

Dynamic Living equals God-given Equipment plus Principles
of Success multiplied by the power of a Proper Self-Image.

This formula forces us to ask the question: What do we really
want out of life? Success? Success is different for many people.
Most people think you can measure success from the amount of
money you accumulate, the degree of fame you achieve, or the
modicum of power you possess. But my definition of success has
little to do with those areas.

Success to me is living dynamically! So here's my definition of
dynamic living. Dynamic living is the kind of life that is filled with
joy and happiness all the time, a life free of fear, free of worry,
continually in the process of achieving worthwhile goals. It is

totally well adjusted in life's six major areas: business, home, social, physical, mental, and spiritual.

At this point the skeptics sit back, arms crossed, and either verbalize or think the doubter's creed: "It won't work," or "Convince me." At the close of a seminar a lady marched up to me, and said, "I listened to you until 3:30 yesterday, and I was so sick of it I had to go home. All that baloney about a life filled with joy and happiness all the time just doesn't work. I tried it once and I know."

Another verbal bullet was shot by a man who said, "You're a Pollyanna. You tiptoe through the tulips of life like nothing ever goes wrong."

Now, I realize there are problems. Sometimes you feel that your problems are too serious to be called challenges; most people think their problems are worse than anyone else's. Job expressed their feeling, "For man is born for trouble, as sparks fly upward."

We all have difficulties. However, in the midst of any situation, it is still possible to be filled with joy and happiness. The problem for many of us is that we like the way it feels to be depressed; people sympathize with us, and that feels good. We love to have other people tell us how rough we have it. But wallowing around in the pits doesn't bring happiness, or solve the problems. A better approach is to be in control in the midst of circumstances. Don't cry about the problems trying to get sympathy; see the good in every situation.

A couple from Texas wrote us after attending a Dynamic Living Seminar and said:

"You probably know that our home burned while we were at the Tyler seminar. We lost all of our material possessions, but we have gained so much more! The day we gazed at the ruined remains I kept remembering, 'You can live a life filled with joy and happiness all the time,' and that thought kept us going. We know that God wants us to live that kind of a life, therefore we also know that He has more in store for us than we can even imagine. The fire chief told us there was no way we could have gotten out alive. Realizing that, we believe that in sparing our lives, God didn't intend for us to spend time crying about what we had lost."

Those friends faced some real problems; however, they chose to face them and work toward the solution. Life is jammed with problems, but the way we handle our problems is the standard which determines whether we live *under* the circumstances or *on top* of them.

I know there are times in life when it is appropriate to be serious. However, underlying everything is a foundation of joy. If one understands the purpose of the challenges of life, and how to handle problems when they come, then happiness is a possibility! Challenges come to reveal a need for change and/or to provide an opportunity for growth.

Let me share a problem-solving process that has been very helpful to me in handling difficult situations.

The steps to problem-solving are (1) Face the fact that there is a problem; (2) Describe it; (3) State the solution and begin to act on it; (4) Never talk about the problem again, only the solution.

Let's take a brief look at these steps. First, there is no way that I know of to solve a problem if you do not recognize its existence. There is nothing wrong with having problems in life. And yes, from time to time there are small challenges which are better off ignored. But sometimes it is important to face the fact that there is a problem.

Perhaps you know the experience of the husband who asks his wife, "What's the matter, honey?" With the coldness of the arctic, the upward tilt of the head and tight lips, she responds, "Nothing." Or perhaps you can relate to the plight of the concerned parent whose teenager rushes in, dashes upstairs, and slams the door, only to respond to the question, "What's wrong?" with a, "Nothing," which can scarcely be understood through the sobs. There is just no way anyone can solve a problem while insisting that nothing is wrong.

Once you have admitted there is something amiss in your life, move quickly to define and state exactly what it is. Time, energy, and emotions are totally wasted on trying to solve the vague generality that "something is wrong." In counseling, I have frequently probed with questions such as, "What's wrong? When did it start? What do you feel happened?" only to hear the nonproductive response, "I don't know." People frequently suffer under the pangs of stress for extended periods of time, simply because they are not willing to isolate and describe the problem.

I believe it is important, as part of the optimistic approach to life, to understand that there is a solution to every problem you face. And when you verbalize the solution, a part of that process is to begin to act upon your statement. Action may reveal the need for an adjustment to the solution, but you'll never solve it if you continue trying to get every detail of the solution proven before you move. Although it may seem impossible, choose a course of action and begin.

The final step in handling problems is the point at which most of us get in trouble. Never, ever, never, never, ever, never, ever (that's almost an absolute) talk about the problem again! Frequently I see people who are really not looking for a solution, but are just looking for someone else to whom they can tell the problem. There are many dangers on that road. Not only do we fail to solve the problem, but talking about it repeatedly tends to amplify and make it worse. "If you think it was bad last week, wait 'til you hear what happened this week!"

Once you have determined the best possible solution and begin your course of action, speak only of that solution. Avoid rehashing the same old problem.

Many of us dwell on our problems so long that the solution is wiped out in the process. It is possible to choose a different course of action. We can choose a life of joy and happiness, a life free of fear and worry. Abraham Lincoln said, "Happiness is a state of mind. A person is as happy as he makes up his mind to be."

But you say, "How can I be happy when I'm so worried about what's going to happen to the world?" Or, "Listen, Ross, you don't know my problems."

My answer is: happiness is a choice, an option in life given to each of us.

Since dynamic living is the kind of a life that is filled with joy and happiness all the time, a life free of fear and worry, I think it will be helpful to take a brief look at three major aspects of fear and worry. It's not my purpose to have you focus on your fears, since I believe that those things you center your thoughts upon are the very things that happen to you. However, as I began to understand fear and worry, and define them, some answers began to emerge.

Healthy vs. Unhealthy Fears

Of course there are sound, healthy fears and concerns, like the consequences of playing hop-scotch on railroad ties with a fast train approaching. Most of us know the right objects and events to hold in "healthy respect"; however, the real worry comes when we choose to dwell on unhealthy or imaginary fears.

Creations of the Imagination

The first thing we should know about fear and worry is that for the most part they are creations of our imagination. This does not mean that the fear is not very real, but it does mean that we may have inflicted it upon ourselves or conjured it as the result of some past experience.

The story of the tired traveler is one example. A man was driving through the northern part of the country and became so exhausted he knew he had to stop. He wanted to pull over to the side of the road and go to sleep, but it was very cold, and he knew it would be dangerous to leave the engine of his car running just so the heater would operate.

He pulled into the first town and wearily tramped into a small hotel. "Sorry, sir," he was told by the clerk, "there isn't a room to be had. The weather is bad and everyone on the road seems to have stopped here." The traveler found another run-down motel; it didn't matter what the place was like, he had to get some sleep.

"Full up," the proprietor said as he slammed the door against the cold blast of air.

At the last place displaying a "no vacancy" sign he sat down. His body ached with weariness, he pleaded with the clerk, "I don't care where you put me . . . if there's space on the floor, I'll sleep there."

"We have a small area that was a storage closet, but we've just done some remodeling, and I guess we could squeeze a rollaway bed in it."

They moved in a small cot and the traveler flopped down on it, grateful for some rest. But he couldn't sleep. The room was closed in and he suffered from claustrophobia. There were no lights in the tight space and he began to feel his way around the room, groping to find a window or transom to let in some air. The walls seemed to move in on him, his throat became tight with fear. He had to find a window. Then his hands pressed against the wall and found a locked door. Inside this small closet he began probing again. He felt an opening, but the window was nailed shut. Panic gripped his chest; he had to have air or he would die. He took off his shoe, and swinging as hard as he could, broke out the bottom pane of the window. With a weary, relieved sigh, he fell on the cot and went sound asleep.

The next morning he opened his eyes and discovered that the window which had given him openness and fresh air was not a window to the outside at all. During the remodeling process it had been sealed in with a solid brick wall. Nothing had changed in his situation, except what he perceived in his mind. His fears were creations of his own imagination, leading to a solution which he thought solved his dilemma.

Source of "I'm Afraid"

If most fear is imaginary, where did it come from in the first place?

Child psychologists tell me that two of the basic fears of childhood are fear of loud noises and fear of falling. So what do we do with our babies? We play little games like "hanky over the face." Our big, grinning faces come within inches of that wide-eyed little one, and at just the right moment we lift the hanky and shout, "Boo!" The child is scared out of his wits, but the big face staring right into his is laughing! Next, the child learns to play our game and puts the cloth over his head, waiting for us to grab it away. He anticipates fear, but is being taught that he cannot express this emotion, because the person with the big face teaches him to laugh. All negative emotions, whether planned or accidentally created, are shoved into the subconscious mind and stored there. What do you think happens when a small child is thrown into the air and caught just before he crashes on the floor? He gasps, his eyes bug out, but there is that face again, laughing away. He is being taught to push the fear into the subconscious where it may emerge later in fear of heights, fear of flying, or some other common phobia.

Someone said, "Are you saying not to play these harmless games with my kids?" No, but as parents we need to recognize that we can teach without realizing it. Some parents use fear as a disciplinary tool. Respect and discipline are requisites in child-raising, but too often in the heat of emotion we are inclined to say or do irrational things. "You do that one more time, and I'll knock your block off," says Mom or Dad, perhaps not realizing this is a fear-producing mechanism.

At our youth camp the young people are very attentive when I tell them about my childhood fears. I explain that sometimes fear and worry are extensions of frightening experiences in childhood, not brought on by parents, but from circumstances. When I talk about being afraid of the dark, the youngsters are glued to their seats, nodding their heads in agreement.

I remember when I was about six or seven years old, my mother had just tucked me in bed and listened to my prayers. She switched out the light, and I stared at the ceiling for a while before turning my head to glance out my window. As I looked through the venetian blinds I stared straight into the face of a man who was peering in my room. I began to scream, but no one could hear me because my throat seemed paralyzed. I jumped out of bed, raced into the living room and shouted to my dad. He ran outside and saw the footprints in the dirt beneath my window, but no one was there.

Another time in my young life my parents had guests and were chatting in the dining room. I came out of the bathroom and looked down the hall to see a man I didn't know inside of my parent's bedroom. The coats and purses of the guests were on the bed and he was rummaging through them. I screamed again, but no sound came out, so I ran into the dining room. The men jumped up and chased the burglar across the lawn, but he had a head start and escaped.

For years I lived with those two experiences of childhood. I began to do things that helped me cope with my fears. Now I didn't go around with a big sign which said, "Filled with fear," but I never went into a room alone if it was dark. If the switch was slightly out of reach I managed to bend around the door frame and stretch to flick on the lights, without moving my body from the safety of a bright hall. Even in my teenage years, I was still afraid of the dark. Just driving in dark neighborhoods was a frightening experience.

Have you ever thought you heard someone walking in the hall, or moving about in the other room? A footstep, a rustle of papers, a squeak of a door sent the shivers down your spine. Then you turned on the light to discover that it was the cat, or maybe just the wind. In our minds, though, we create pictures that frighten us. But most of the things we fear are imaginary, because of things that have happened to us which have created the fear.

Fear thoughts are planted in the subconscious in many ways: parents who use fear to discipline, who deliberately or ignorantly begin building little fears, frightening childhood experiences, horror movies or scary television programs, or books filled with frightening imagery.

Whether fears are imaginary, results of experiences, or taught, we know they are there. Emerson said, "He has not learned the lesson of life who does not every day surmount a fear."

Fear and Worry Are Highly Destructive

The expression, "worried to death," has more truth in it than you might think. Studies are being done on the elderly to see how many of them die as a result of the fear of crime that stalks in vulnerable neighborhoods. Fear can be paralyzing, as well as fatal. This story of the man in the box car is one illustration. It was quitting time for the train crew. Accidentally, one of the men was locked in a refrigerator box car, and the remainder of the workmen left the site; the man inside knew that no one would be around until morning.

He banged and shouted until his fists were bloody and his voice was hoarse: No one heard him. *If I can't get out, I'll freeze to death in here*, he thought.

Finding a knife, he began to etch words on the wooden floor. He wrote, "It's so cold, my body is getting numb . . . if I could just go to sleep . . . these may be my last words."

The next morning the crew slid open the heavy doors of the freight car and found him dead. An autopsy revealed that every physical sign of his body indicated he had frozen to death. And yet the refrigeration unit of the car was inoperative, and the temperature inside indicated fifty-five degrees. He had killed himself by the power of his fear.

Another story is about a couple of high-school kids who were high on hallucinatory drugs. One of the boys said to his friend, "Listen, guy, I'm gonna get you. See this gun here. I'm just gonna shove this into your gut and pull the trigger." With those brash, but false words he stuck his finger into the other boy's chest and said, "Bang." The boy fell to the ground, dead.

Because of the unusual circumstances, no gun, no wound, an autopsy was ordered and revealed that his heart had exploded in the place where his companion poked his finger, just as if he had been shot with a bullet. High on drugs, hallucinating, fear was intensified and caused the death.

If most fears are imaginary, and fear and worry are highly destructive, we reach the logical question, "What do we do?" I don't know how you're going to handle these feelings, but I know how I did it.

Curing and Killing Fear

How do we find a way to handle fear and worry? Many people say action will kill fear. That's true. I believe it, teach it, and practice it. There's a little boy named Kenny who may never realize how he has been used to illustrate this principle.

The first year our camp opened, we were lacking in sports equipment, so we were looking for something energetic for the kids to do. We discovered that some enterprising individuals had built an exciting water ride down a steep slope on one of our Michigan mountains. They had a series of little sleds which were attached to a track and zoomed down a curving course, picking up speed as they went.

We took about thirty of the kids up a ski lift to reach the start of the ride and had them line up for the thrilling descent. They thought tobogganing in the summer was a real adventure.

However, I watched this one little guy get close to the front of the line and then quietly slip out and go to the end. He did this about four times until it was time for all of us to go home, and he still hadn't gone down the hill. I said, "It's your turn, Kenny, let's go."

"Well, Mr. Ross, I think I'll just wait it out this time . . . I can go some other day."

"Kenny, everybody's having a blast. Come on, you'll love it."

"Oh, no, Mr. Ross, I think I'll just walk down."

"Sorry, Kenny, can't do that. It's too steep, and besides, all the other kids would have to wait for you. Come on, let's go."

We parried back and forth; I cajoled, he balked; I encouraged, he refused. All the time he was wiggling his arms out of his sweater and when I wasn't looking he wadded it up and stuffed it in the side of his shirt. With his best pained expression he said, "I can't go . . . see, Mr. Ross, I'm sick. I've got a big lump in my side."

Half pulling, half carrying, I propelled him onto the toboggan, sat down in back of him with my legs wrapped around his body and my arms holding his chest, and we were pushed off. Kenny screamed, "No, no, stop, help," until we were about fifty feet down and banking a curve when the words changed to, "Wheeee!" We hit the bottom and Kenny leaped out, grabbed my arm and shouted, "Come on, Mr. Ross, let's go again!"

Sometimes action is a step-by-step process to handle our fears and worries. A survey was taken that revealed that forty-one percent of the people polled were most afraid of speaking in public. Since communication is necessary to achieve success in many fields, I believe it should be taught gradually, not by shoving someone before a crowd of a thousand people.

In our business, for instance, it is necessary to meet new people all the time, to talk with them and get to know them. When we have a new associate who is afraid of meeting people we say, "Go to a shopping mall and walk around, smile and say 'hi.' Don't stop or you may have to carry on a conversation. But when you're comfortable doing that, advance to saying, 'Hi, how are you doing?' and stop. Who knows, you may make a friend. There are thousands of people who are starved for someone to notice them."

However, action alone will not cure all your fear and worry. Much of it is buried at a deep subconscious level and action never touches it. Therefore, we need to find a way to handle fear at that level. The only way that I know is to place those thoughts into the subconscious mind that will dilute the effect of all the fearful thoughts which have been programmed into us throughout our lives.

Because the Scriptures were meaningful in my life, I took two Bible verses and put them together. And whenever fear would come into my life I repeated those verses over and over. Most of the time I would say them out loud, and as often as I could, to myself in a mirror. The Old Testament verse is:

"And so we need not fear even if the world blows up, and the mountains crumble into the sea" (Psalm 46:2, TLB).

The New Testament reference is: "God hath not given us the spirit of fear, but of power, and of love, and of a sound mind" (2 Timothy 1:7, KJV).

Sometimes I would repeat those verses for as long as an hour, until I began to handle the fears which were so much a part of my life.

Maybe you have to make up a statement of your own to begin to handle your fear. A friend used this statement: "Fear knocked at the door, faith answered, and no one was there." Whatever works for you—use it.

Goals Are Not for Fools

The next part of my definition for dynamic living is not a final element, it is a process. Dynamic living is continually in the process of accomplishing worthwhile goals.

Most of us are not encouraged to begin to set goals early in life. Have you ever heard someone say to a junior high or high school young person, "Don't worry about what you're going to do with your life; you'll change your mind fifteen hundred times before you get out of school anyhow, so don't worry about it"?

I understand that approach and philosophy, but I don't agree with it. Some of the dreams and desires that kids have become lifetime purposes and goals; they can be accomplished, wild as they may appear.

John Goddard had one of the most dramatic records of personal purposes and goals in modern times. His story was published in *Life* magazine in 1972. He was fifteen years old when he over-heard his grandmother and aunt saying, "If only I had done this when I was young." Goddard resolved not to be a part of the army of "if onlys" and so he sat down and decided what he wanted to do with his life. He wrote down 127 goals. He listed ten rivers he wanted to explore, seventeen mountains he wanted to climb. He wanted to have a career in medicine, visit every country in the world, learn to fly an airplane, retrace the travels of Marco Polo, ride a horse in the Pasadena Rose Parade. Other goals were to read the Bible from cover to cover, read the works of Shakespeare, Plato, Aristotle, Dickens, and a dozen other classic authors. He wanted to become an Eagle Scout, dive in a submarine, play the flute and violin, go on a church mission, marry and have children (he had five), and read the entire *Encyclopaedia Britannica*.

In 1972, John Goddard was forty-seven years old and 103 of his 127 goals had become a reality. As a result, he became a highly paid lecturer and toured the world telling of his adventures.

Setting goals and pursuing them is exciting!

Setting Goals Backwards

Most people set goals on the basis of their past record. They look at what they did in the past, whether they were successful or unsuccessful, and then establish goals on what they think they can do. That's the wrong way!

Remember what the Bible says about Jesus? It says that he set his face to go to Jerusalem. He had a goal and looked ahead, not back on previous experiences.

What we need to do in the process of goal-setting is to decide what we want—what we want to do or be—and then set the goal. Don't look at the past; when we set goals on the basis of yesterday's experience we limit the future by the past. That's backwards.

We Are Goal-Oriented Creatures

When the goal is set and you commit yourself to that goal, you will find a way to make it become reality. When John Goddard was fifteen, he was not an expert mountain climber, a skilled scuba diver, nor an accomplished photographer. However, because he had set goals he found the talent and ability to develop all those skills in order to accomplish what he set out to do when he was a teenager.

Success: Destination or Journey?

It is not simply setting one goal and accomplishing it that gives meaning and zest to life. Too many times a person will set the goal, reach it, and then bask in the accomplishment. It's like the writer with one best seller, the actor who starred in one movie, or the business person who landed one contract.

Unfortunately, we are not taught much about goal-setting or success principles in school. This fact surfaced one time when a graduating class at Harvard University was asked, "Is success a destination or a journey?" Out of 1100 seniors, over 930 answered, "Success is a destination; it is something you know you have when you possess enough money, achieve fame or a certain position."

I don't agree with that philosophy. Success is a journey. If we understand that, then we realize that goals must be set continually.

To be without a goal is to die psychologically.

Balance Is the Key

The final element in dynamic living is making the application of the principles to every area of life. To continue in the process of accomplishing worthwhile goals would be aimless if we become lopsided human beings. Balance is the key. There are six major areas of life: business, home, social, physical, mental, and spiritual (not listed in order of importance). When I conduct business seminars, I specifically emphasize business goals. However, we cannot isolate the goals in any one area of our lives and live dynamically.

A man went to a seminar on business goals and was told that if he would apply the principles taught there he would double his insurance business. He listened carefully and went home and began to utilize what he had been taught. Before long his insurance business doubled, then tripled and quadrupled. The money was rolling in! In fact, there was finally enough money for his wife to afford an attorney, divorce him and take his money with her! Many people find this story amusing at first. But it is tragic when we understand what really happened. In the process of fulfilling his business goals he forgot he had a family. The same principles which brought business success would have developed an exciting family experience if applied at home. His values were out of balance.

In 1923, nine of the most highly successful men in the world had a meeting at the Edgewater Beach Hotel in Chicago. Those men controlled more wealth than the United States government did at that time. They had learned the application of success principles in their business experience. However, twenty-five years later, three of those men were totally broke, bankrupt. Another three were not only broke, but in a penitentiary. The last three had committed suicide. Here were nine of the most highly successful men in the world, as most people count success, and yet a quarter of a century later they had nothing. So what really is success?

One of the wealthiest men in our time spent the last four years of his life living alone in a hotel room in his shorts, on a bed, watching closed-circuit television movies. He had controlled billions of dollars, and yet he made his servants put paper towels on the floor between his bed and the bathroom so he would not have to walk on the rug and get contaminated. He was served food in utensils sealed in plastic pouches, so they would be completely germ-free. This man learned the application of the principles of business, but forgot he had a home life, a social life, a spiritual, mental, and physical life.

There are many wealthy people across our country who would say, "I'd give everything I've got if I could just have my health back," or, "I'd give up my fortune if I could just have my family back!"

So the first part of the Magic Formula is DL . . . Dynamic Living!

Dynamic living is that kind of life that's filled with joy and happiness all the time. It's free of fear, free of worry. It's continually in the process of accomplishing worthwhile goals and is totally well adjusted in life's six major areas: business, home, social, physical, mental, and spiritual.

Impossible? Not at all. God has given us the equipment to achieve that kind of living. "Who, me?" Yes, every single one of you have the God-given equipment to achieve whatever you want. Edgar Guest, who was called "the poet of the plain people," wrote the kind of verses that encourage us to believe in our potential.

EQUIPMENT

Figure it out for yourself, my lad,
You've all that the greatest of men have had,
Two arms, two hands, two legs, two eyes,
And a brain to use if you would be wise.
With this equipment they all began,
So start for the top and say, "I can."

Look them over, the wise and great,
They take their food from a common plate,
And similar knives and forks they use,

With similar laces they tie their shoes,
The world considers them brave and smart,
But you've all they had when they made their start.

You can triumph and come to skill,
You can be great if you only will.
You're well equipped for what fight you choose,
You have legs and arms and a brain to use,
And the man who has risen great deeds to do,
Began his life with no more than you.

You are the handicap you must face,
You are the one who must choose your place,
You must say where you want to go,
How much you will study the truth to know.
God has equipped you for life, but He
Lets you decide what you want to be.

Courage must come from the soul within,
The man must furnish the will to win.
So figure it out for yourself, my lad,
You were born with all that the great have had,
With your equipment they all began.
Get hold of yourself, and say: "I can."*

---

*Reprinted from *Collected Verses of Edgar A. Guest,* © 1934 by Edgar A. Guest, with the permission of Contemporary Books, Inc., Chicago, IL.

3

YOU ARE A GENIUS

What are you worth? Scientists at one time determined that the chemicals within our bodies were worth about ninety-nine cents. With inflation, that may have increased to $2.50 or more. Viewed another way, it is estimated that the energy production of the human body, based upon the number of atoms within a 150-pound person, could generate enough atomic energy to be valued at $85 billion! That's more like it!

Just what are you really worth, not in dollars, but in personal power? Society columnists talk about "the beautiful people" and mean the socially prominent, famous, or wealthy. Television and radio commentators interview "special people" or have a story about a "unique person." But it is important for each of us to accept the fact that we are beautiful, special, unique, and have extremely high value. God created us and has equipped us with certain talents and individuality. This is part of the magic formula which is called GGE . . . *God-given Equipment*.

I also believe we are all geniuses. Albert Einstein, a man who achieved some of the greatest intellectual breakthroughs in history, was quoted as saying that the average person uses two percent of his intellectual capacity. That's not very much!

Many of us have been denying our own potential since we were small children—not believing what we ought to believe about ourselves. We have allowed others, and particularly ourselves, to put us down.

We have talents and abilities that are untapped. We look at the complexities of modern computers and are amazed! And yet current study in human capacity shows far greater potential in the human mind.

"The human brain is remarkably compact. It weighs only about 50 ounces in the average adult male and about 5 ounces less in the average woman. It requires only about 1/10 volt of electricity to perform efficiently, yet it is composed of literally tens of billions of nerve cells. Although the brain operates both less rapidly and less accurately than a computer, it leaves even the most advanced computer far behind in its truly staggering capacity. The network of interconnections (called synapses) between the billions of nerve cells (neurons) in the brain is potentially able to process information bits in ways whose number is equivalent to 2 to the 10^{13}. This is a number considerably greater than the total of all the atoms in the entire universe! Yet so neatly packaged is the human brain that in order even to approach such a capacity, a modern computer would have to be at least 10,000 times larger than the average brain" (*Psychofeedback,* p. 33).

Your Personal Computer

The computer which you possess within could cost as much as ten billion dollars to build, and yet it's right in your cranial cavity. What a potential!

We live in an age which is becoming more comfortable with computers all the time. We even speak in terms of the "personal computer." The capacity of these small machines is astounding, but when we consider our potential there is no comparison.

"Neurologists have estimated that about two million signals or stimuli come into the central nervous system every second. Of course, you do not perceive all of those two million per second inputs. A series of discriminating "filters" send most of the incoming signals to parts of the brain which process and use that

information automatically, without your conscious attention"
(*Release Your Brakes,* p. 46).

This process of receiving, filtering, and storing data began before we were even born. All of this stored information and instructions have formed "programs," or what might be referred to as
habit patterns. Most of what we do is a matter of habit. This
programming process can be controlled and changed, but it operates all the time and continues until the day we die.

Dr. Gordon Shepherd, professor of physiology at Yale, writes
in his book, *The Synaptic Organization of the Brain:* "It is com-
monplace to cite an estimate of ten billion neurons. Those who cite
this figure invariably fail to recall or realize that the number of
granule cells in the cerebellum is probably several times this
number."

Everything that has happened to you up to this particular point in
your life . . . the things you do, the movements you make, the
thoughts you think, the things you sense (see, smell, taste, hear,
and touch), have been permanently recorded in your subconscious
mind.*

Convincing Evidence of Your Genius

Do you need convincing? This story may never occur exactly as
related here, but when you admit that something similar has happened to you on many occasions, you should be convinced that
you are a genius.

----

*Much discussion continues in technical circles about the validity of using
the term "subconscious" mind to describe mental activity which happens without your conscious awareness or direction. There are many who believe "unconscious" area of the brain is more accurate. We now have convincing evidence there is a small part of our brain which can be called the physical basis of
the mind consciousness. Two outstanding physiologists discussed it and
named it the "Reticular Activating System." Dr. G. Moruzzi and Dr. H. W.
Magaun wrote of it in the book, *The Waking Brain.* It is the only part of the
brain which connects with every other part of the brain and the rest of the body
and ceases all activity whenever we lose consciousness. We have chosen,
however, because this is not a technical treatise, to use the term "subconscious," because of its common usage and wide popular understanding.

A young man is walking down the street when he sees a very important person approaching him. He thinks, *Today is the day I must ask that question of this person.* He begins to formulate the question in his mind; he wants to say precisely the right words and use the proper facial and body expressions. The question must be posed exactly right because he wants "yes" for an answer.

As they approach one another, he is thinking, *What shall I say and how shall I say it?*

She's in front of him now, they say "Hi" and exchange small talk. Then he decides the time is right to ask that very important question.

"Mary, I want to ask. . . ."

He gets five words out of his mouth when something inside says, "Stop!"

Why did he end his sentence in mid-air? There is a communication process from the subconscious mind to the conscious mind. Everything that has ever happened in your lifetime is permanently recorded in the subconscious mind. The subconscious relays signals to the conscious mind in a mysterious manner; some people call it a hunch, a sixth sense, intuition, or programming. Others say it's a "still, small voice."

When the young man stops his question, his conscious mind and subconscious mind carry on an unspoken conversation.

The conscious mind says, "What do you mean, 'Stop?' "

The subconscious mind answers, "Because, if you continue to go ahead and ask the question, you will get 'no' for an answer."

Conscious and Subconscious converse back and forth several times until the selection of words and sentences has been run through the computer and the sixth word that comes out of the young man's mouth is exactly the right one for the situation.

The entire communication process takes place as fast as you can snap your fingers, and Mary never knows the complicated procedure that has just taken place.

Hasn't that type of thing happened to you sometime in your life? Who else but a genius could have that type of communication exchange completed in split seconds?

Sometimes the message from that still, small voice (or whatever we want to call it) is ignored. We don't pay any attention to it and go ahead and stick our foot in our mouth. We've all done it. We say the wrong word, make the wrong move, in spite of our inner feelings.

However, all of us have had the experience of responding to some special urgings that have been important messages for our lives. A person of faith, who knows the Lord in a personal way, will attribute these directions to Divine Guidance. My father was one of those persons.

The Right Ticket

My father, a minister, was scheduled for a meeting in Akron, Ohio. We were living in California, and he went to the airport late one Sunday night after evening service to board an airplane to fly to Akron for the beginning of an evangelistic service. He boarded the plane, the doors were closed, and they were ready to take off. They were moving the stairway back when suddenly he stood up, went to the stewardess, and said, "I've got to get off this plane right now."

He spoke with such conviction that she didn't argue. The stairway was brought back, the door opened, and my dad got off that plane.

He went straight to the train station, bought a ticket, and for four days traveled across the country to get to Ohio. When he arrived, the pastor of the local church picked him up and after they had chatted for a while he said, "By the way, did you hear about the plane that went down? A flight out of Los Angeles left on Sunday night and crashed into the side of a mountain. Everyone on board was killed."

Yes, it was the same plane my father left, because "something" had told him to get off and go by train.

The Genius of the Human Mind

Potentially, all of you are geniuses. That's the way you were created. You have different ways of expressing yourselves, different talents and abilities.

Someone challenged me by saying, "What about the mentally retarded? You talk as if everybody is a genius. That can't be possible."

Recently I was introduced to the work of a doctor who decided that children with Down's Syndrome could learn how to function adequately in our society. He took twenty-five of these youngsters and began to teach them. He began with the alphabet; it took him over 4,000 repetitions of the letter "A" before they could recognize and repeat that letter. Then he moved on to the next letters. Eventually, the number of repetitions decreased to about 2,000, and then to 900 and gradually to about 400. Finally, he showed them a letter just once and they could recognize it.

Every one of those twenty-five D.S. children entered public high school and graduated. One of them graduated with top scholastic honors in his class.

Amazing things happen if you begin to believe in your potential.

A couple of teachers took a group of mentally retarded children scoring 30 to 40 on IQ tests and told those kids how beautiful they were, how talented they were, and how much they could do. The teachers repeated this over and over again. The school authorities countered with the idea, "Look, be kind to them, make them comfortable and happy, but they'll never amount to much in life."

But the teachers refused to accept that as a statement of reality and continued to tell those children how great they were. Those kids are in high school today, scoring between 130 and 140 on IQ tests.

One of the young men who attended our ranch had been programmed to believe he could never achieve above average grades. One counselor after another told him he would never get anything above a "C." Problems of adjustment, frustrations, psychological counseling—they all ended in what appeared to be a fulfillment of what he had been told. Then I told him he was potentially a genius. Now he had to make a choice—"Whom shall I believe?" I'm happy to tell you that this past year he made the Dean's Honor Roll! They said it couldn't be done, but he did it!

Of Course You're a Genius

You have tens of billions of brain cells. Every one of those cells is capable of receiving and storing pieces of information. It has been said that the human mind is capable of two million impressions per second, twenty-four hours a day, seventy-five years in a row, without the slightest hint of fatigue. But most of us suffer from tired feelings at one time or another; we drag through life exhausted. Why? Later we'll talk about energy leaks that occur in life, but first let's contemplate the mental potential we have.

In these days of national debt and gigantic corporations, the term "billion" is an indifferent amount. However, a billion is a lot! If you had a billion dollars to go on a buying spree and spent ten thousand dollars every day you would be shopping for three hundred years!

What do we do with this mental potential? William James, the father of modern psychology in America, said the average person uses about 10 percent of his overall capacities. Even the best among us uses only about 15 percent. What if you and I could be challenged to use just 20, even 25 percent of what we already have? We could turn the world upside down! It's wonderful to see what happens when people begin to say "yes" to their potential. Often that great potential within each one of us is summoned at the point of crisis—very seldom at any other time.

In the realm of God-given equipment we are richly endowed.

You Have a Perfect Memory

You might say, "Oh, come on. I can't even remember four items on a shopping list! What do you mean a perfect memory?"

We have perfect memories; it's recall that sometimes gives us the challenge.

One of Canada's leading neurosurgeons, Dr. Wilder Penfield, has done some brilliant research in the field of memory. In *Speech and Brain Mechanisms,* Dr. Penfield speaks of his work in stimulating the brain electrically. He discovered that when the brain is stimulated a person can relive an experience from an earlier time.

"A young man, JT, who had recently come from his home in South Africa, cried out when the superior surface of his right temporal lobe was being stimulated, 'Yes, Doctor . . . now I hear people laughing . . . my friends in South Africa.' After stimulation was over, he could discuss his double awareness and express his astonishment, for it had seemed to him that he was with his cousins at their home where he and the two young ladies were laughing together. This was an experience from his earlier life. It had faded from his recollective memory, but the ganglionic pattern which must have been formed during that experience was still intact and available to the stimulating electrode. It was at least as clear to him as it would have been had he closed his eyes and ears thirty seconds after the event and rehearsed the whole scene 'from memory' " (*Speech and Brain Mechanisms* pp. 45, 46).

A few years ago the headlines contained a dramatic illustration of our perfect memory capabilities. On July 16, 1976, at Chowchilla, California, a vicious crime was committed by three men. A school bus with twenty-six children between the ages of five and fourteen and their driver, was stopped on a lonely country road by armed men wearing masks. The men kidnaped the children and the bus driver, hurried them into two closed vans, and drove them miles away to a quarry. Throughout the eleven-hour trip the kidnapers rarely spoke. At the quarry the children and the bus driver, Ed Ray, were imprisoned in an old moving van that was buried six feet underground.

Sixteen hours after first entering the pit, Ray managed to force open a small ventilation cover in the roof of the van and the captives were able to squeeze out.

Police issued bulletins for three males traveling in two vans, but they weren't found. The driver and children were unable to describe the men, and Ed Ray had only noticed the license plate on one of the vans briefly, but he couldn't remember the number.

After hours of questioning the victims, and then weeks of fruitless investigation, there were still no clues to the identity of the kidnapers.

Then Sheriff Ed Bates, who was in charge of the case, remembered that the Los Angeles Police Department had used hypnosis to solve a number of crimes when victims or witnesses were unable to remember details. Ed Ray was hypnotized, and in a state of hypnosis he repeated the license plate number of one of the vans. He was correct to one digit. Within an hour the police were at the home of the owner of that van, who was, of course, one of the kidnapers.

How long do you think Ed Ray looked at the plate number? Probably only a moment. But when he saw it, his mind said with intensity, ''I must remember.'' When all of the blocks were taken away, the subconscious mind was able to release the information that had been stored there.

Perhaps you have heard stories of people who have photographic memories. They read a book and remember what page contained a certain story, or the location on a page of some statistics. You may have thought that talent was for a select few, but too often we do not use that talent because we have denied our abilities in this area.

Have you ever said, ''I can remember faces, but I can't remember names''? It is possible to develop the capacity to remember. If you choose to do so, you can develop the ability to meet several hundred people in a short period of time and be able to recall every person sometime later. Today there are people who do seminars on how to train your mind to use the God-given equipment for memory that you already possess. One fellow, Jerry Lucas, used to memorize pages of the New York City telephone directory just to hone his memory ability. He has now applied these techniques to Scripture memorization and can quote whole books of the Bible. It is possible to develop that kind of memory.

What is your reading capacity? I have heard people say, ''I'm such a slow reader, I just can't seem to get through a book.'' Most people read somewhere between 200 to 300 words a minute. And yet it is possible to develop 3,000 to 4,000 words a minute reading capability. I have a business associate in Southern California who recently tested at 7,500 words per minute with 85 percent comprehension. This man developed part of his capacity to a greater extent than most of us do.

What about you? What are you doing with the God-given equipment which you have? Have you said, "Yes" to your potential, or are you using five to ten percent of it?

A Forest of Giants

We may never know what our abilities are, mental or physical, until put to trial.

When I was going to college, I had a friend who had never trained for weight-lifting. That sport demands self-discipline, and men train for years breaking down muscle and building it up so they can grab those weights and shove them over their heads. My muscles are challenged just thinking about that amount of weight.

My friend was coming back to college from Christmas vacation, driving from Seattle, Washington, to Santa Barbara, California, traveling rather fast through central California on a three-lane road. He and his fiancée had determined to drive twenty-four hours, nonstop, in order to get back to classes on Monday morning.

In the early hours of the morning, fog and mist swirling around the winding road, there was very little traffic. They hadn't passed a home or a car in miles. Suddenly they came upon a curve that was not well-marked. The road was slippery and as they hit that curve, the car couldn't hold the road; it skidded, flipped over, and began to roll.

The young man was thrown out of the car. He hit the ground, dazed by the impact, but was able to get to his feet, only to see his car continue to roll and come to a stop, upside down. He ran to his car and discovered the girl he loved was trapped underneath. He looked around frantically for help and shouted into the still night. There was no one around. Hot gasoline was pouring out of the engine onto her arms and legs and great blisters were beginning to form. He knew that in a matter of moments she would be dead. There was only one thing he could possibly do.

He reached down, grabbed the bumper of a car that weighed over 2,000 pounds and lifted it from her so that she could roll out from underneath.

I have been utterly amazed when someone comes to me after a

seminar with this statement that exudes a lack of appreciation for faith in God-given equipment: "Yes, but that was only adrenaline!"

My answer is, "Yes, isn't that marvelous? That's the whole point."

More Than Adrenaline

A good friend of mine, Merrill Womack, was traveling from Southern California to Spokane, Washington, the day before Thanksgiving, 1961, in his twin-engine plane. He was a skilled pilot who had over 1,500 hours of solo flight experience. Over northern Oregon he was forced by severe weather to find a small airport and spend the night. The next morning, a cold, clear day, he intended to return home and spend Thanksgiving with his family.

He taxied to the end of the runway, checked all the instruments, and took off. About a quarter of a mile beyond the runway, both engines quit. As a pilot he knew he had two or three choices: one was to find a clear spot and land. There was no clearing. His second choice was to bank the plane and return to the runway. He didn't have enough altitude or power, and as he started to bank, the plane began to shudder. The only choice he had was to look for the place with the fewest number of trees, and crash land. As he hit, the plane exploded upon impact and burst into flames. He had just filled the tanks with 100 gallons of high octane fuel. The heat from that fire was so intense it melted some of the metal parts of the plane. He was dazed inside the cockpit, but conscious; for a few brief moments he realized he would have to get out or be burned alive. With one hand he grabbed the door handle and pushed it open, with the other hand he reached for his safety belt and tried to unlatch it. It was jammed!

He did the only thing that was possible for him to do; he grabbed that airline safety belt and ripped it in half.

But, you say, you can't rip a safety belt in half. Right. But he did. Today he travels all over the country doing concerts, and testifying to the power of our God-given abilities. When he sings, "To God Be the Glory," he knows the truth of those words.

The woman's world record for weight-lifting in what is known as the dead-weight lift is about 400 pounds. Women train their bodies for years to perform such an incredible feat. Let me tell you the story about a little San Diego housewife who weighed about 100 pounds. She was standing on a corner, waiting to cross the street when she heard the sickening sounds of screeching brakes and looked up just in time to see a car hit a little girl, knock her down, and drag her about fifty feet. When the car stopped, its front wheel seemed to be resting on the child's head.

The mother of the little girl ran into the street, screaming for help, but no one was around. The driver of the car was an emotional wreck, because he believed he had killed the little girl. Both of them stood, helpless at the scene of the accident.

The housewife, horrified by what she had just seen, didn't stop to consider her size, the weight of the car, or whether or not she could do anything. She reached under the fender of that heavy vehicle and began to pull. She strained so hard that the metal part of the fender cut through her fingers, but she didn't stop. Finally she lifted the car high enough for the little girl's mother to pull that limp little body out and have her rushed to the hospital.

That child is alive today, because the housewife said "Yes" to her potential. Police who investigated the accident said the car weighed 4,800 pounds!

Polish Your GGE

There are so many things we can do if we use what God gives us! For example, we have a highly successful business associate in Seattle, Washington, who uses the talents he has, although he is totally blind. I watched him conduct a seminar one weekend and marveled at his abilities and humor. As he stood at the podium with a notebook full of notes (in Braille, of course), someone would come up behind him and he would slam the notebook shut and say, "Hey, you can't read my notes."

He would introduce the speakers on the platform, and as he

backed away from the microphone to the edge of the stage, which was about three feet high, he would come to within a quarter of an inch of the edge and stop.

Time after time during the weekend, people would come up to him and say, "Hi, Dick, how are you?" He would stick out his hand, call them by name, and say, "It's great to see you."

One morning Dick and his wife, Dee, took some children for a tour of Seattle. That evening the little boy said to his daddy, "Daddy, we had so much fun this morning, but there's one thing I don't understand. How come Dee drives the car all the time?"

The children had been with them the entire day, but never knew that Dick was blind!

What is our capacity? None of us need to wait for the crisis moments in our lives to realize our potential.

The poet, Robert Browning, said, "My business is not to remake myself, but to make the absolute best of what God made."

Even the minute details of your physical body give testimony to the truth of the statement, "I am fearfully and wonderfully made" (Psalm 139:14, NIV). Genetic biologists now indicate that every cell in our bodies has within it the complete genetic history of our life's experience. That information, if printed out, would fill thirty volumes of the encyclopedia!

Consider now the truth of God's word: "You made all the delicate, inner parts of my body, and knit them together in my mother's womb. Thank you for making me so wonderfully complex! It is amazing to think about. Your workmanship is marvelous—and how well I know it. You were there while I was being formed in utter seclusion! You saw me before I was born and scheduled each day of my life before I began to breathe. Every day was recorded in your Book!" (Psalm 139:13–16, TLB).

God made you a genius with supernatural potential!

GIVE AND YOU RECEIVE

Principle #1: The Principle of Giving
"Give and you will receive."

What would happen if you woke up tomorrow morning, squinted at the clock, and stuck your foot out of bed, not knowing whether it would go up or down? Imagine thinking, *I wonder if my foot will touch the floor or spring toward the ceiling!* Absurd? Yes, because we know there's a law at work which applies to all of us, whether we understand it or not. Gravity is a fact, believe it or not. You can't touch it; can't smell it; can't taste it; can't hear it; but it still exists.

There are certain exact principles in the area of human motivation, success, and failure that have been working in your life ever since you were born, and will continue to work until the day you die. The tragedy that I see in the lives of many people is that they have never been told what the principles are or had explained to them how the principles can be used for their benefit.

Understand how these principles work and you can use them to propel yourself forward into any kind of an experience you choose to have in life. Life is meant to be lived to the utmost!

During the time Susan and I have operated Circle A ranch,

teaching kids between the ages of eleven and eighteen the formula for dynamic living, we have watched these young people go
home and apply the principles and see themselves in a different
perspective. The principles can be applied at any age, to people
from all economic, educational, and social backgrounds. They are
universal. In Ecclesiastes 7:13 we read, "See the way the Creator
does things and fall into line. Don't fight the facts of nature"
(TLB). Glenn Bland, in his fine book, *Success,* commenting on this
matter says, "You can't beat him; many who were more capable
than you and I have tried and failed, so you may as well join him
and let his natural laws work for you and not against you! . . . You
can operate within the framework of these laws, and happiness and
success will be yours for the taking" (p. 43).

Don't get me wrong. I'm not saying I have learned all of these
principles perfectly, nor do I say that you must have all of these
ideas operating in your life to live dynamically. However, the
principles exist, they do work, and if you will try to understand
them and begin to work on them, you will discover that your life
will become a highly exhilarating experience. In these next few
exciting chapters we will speak of ten major principles of successful living. Along with each principle will come a short summary
statement. Begin now to implant these principles and summaries
indelibly in your mind. They will change your life!

The Principle of Giving

The first of these is expressed as the principle of giving. As a
summary statement it says, "Give and you receive." People express this principle in different ways: The law of action and reaction; the law of radiation and attraction; the law of cause and
effect. The Bible speaks about the law of sowing and reaping.

If you plant corn, you get corn. I've never seen radishes grown
from a seed of corn. If you plant barley, you get barley. If you
plant hate, what do you get? If you plant love, what happens?
When standing before a group of a thousand people it's fun to
throw out questions like that and have everyone, college pro-
fessors included, shout back: corn, barley, hate, love, or whatever

we suggest. Until we get to money. Test yourself. What would you say if I asked you what you would get if you planted ten dollar bills? One fellow in a seminar shouted, "Dirty money." Another said, "You get your head examined, dummy!"

I was on a flight into Baltimore, doing some reading and enjoying the time to feed the mental part of my life. About half way through the trip I stuck the book in the pocket in front of my seat so the title was evident. The man sitting next to me commented, "Interesting book," and we started a conversation.

I enjoyed talking with him. He had been a businessman most of his life, but dropped out of the corporate world about three years before to go into the ministry. He went to Bible college, preparing to be a missionary to Africa. He had been traveling around doing deputation work—preaching in services where he tells people what he is going to do and asks for their support. Just before I met him, the last money he and his family needed for the trip to Africa had come in only two days before they were to depart.

"Isn't it wonderful how God provides when we need it?" I commented. And we talked for a few minutes about other experiences of life when something happens just in the nick of time.

All of a sudden something inside of me said, "Give him a hundred dollars." My first reaction to that little voice was, "I don't know a lot about him. How can I be sure he is doing what he is supposed to be doing or not?" The idea persisted: "Give him one hundred dollars." I said to myself, "Wait a minute, he just told me that he received all he needed last Sunday night." But the feeling wouldn't leave me. When we landed in Baltimore, I said to my new acquaintance, "I don't know how you're going to feel about this. We've never met before, but something tells me you're going to need a hundred dollars and I'm supposed to give it to you." I pulled out the cash, handed it to him while his mouth was still open, and got off the plane. I had never seen him before and may never see him again.

Just one week later I was traveling across the country to do a speaking engagement for a business friend. He said he couldn't promise any financial remuneration, maybe not even to cover my travel expenses, but when he told me he needed help, I said, "I'll be there." We had a seminar for about six hours and the next day I flew home. A week later a check came in the mail to cover the travel expenses and a second check for twelve hundred dollars for that speaking engagement, for which I had been promised nothing.

"Hold on, now," you must be saying. "Do you mean to tell me that you think you got a twelve to one return on that hundred you gave away?" Well, the principle is that whatever you give that's what you receive. Sometimes it comes back to you in dramatic ways, other times you may have forgotten your gift (which is commendable) and are pleased when you receive a magnificent return. The Living Bible says, "For if you give, you will get! Your gift will return to you in full and overflowing measure, pressed down, shaken together to make room for more, and running over. Whatever measure you use to give—large or small—will be used to measure what is given back to you" (Luke 6:36).

First Foundation Stone of Giving

If the principle of giving is true, and I happen to believe it is, then there are three corollary statements which are also true. They form the foundation for this powerful principle. The first basis of belief is this: There is no such reality as something for nothing. No free lunch. However, we are being led daily into a mushy swamp of soft thinking which tries to convince us that we can get something for nothing.

A lady received a letter in the mail saying that if she would go to a certain place in Palm Springs and turn in a little coupon she had received in the mail, she would get a prize. She might win ten thousand dollars, the letter said. She drove for two hours in ninety-five degree heat, without air conditioning, and received her "prize": a cheap camera that recorded fuzzy pictures. However, since she had come so far, the salesman said, she must see the wonderful desert land she could buy at such a low price she couldn't afford to turn it down!

In the field of communication, there are subliminal messages which are designed to move us emotionally into believing that we can have something for nothing. Those innocent game shows move our thinking in that direction. Most of the answers are based upon pure chance, not knowledge or skill. The message is simple: if we're lucky, life will deal us the right cards and we'll win the trip, or the car, or whatever.

Las Vegas is jammed with the something for nothing philosophy, as are many other areas of our lives. Zig Ziglar says, "It's ironic, (or is it hypocritical), that responsible people agree with the 'no free lunch' and 'you can't get something for nothing' philosophy, but often vote for legalized gambling, horse racing, dog racing, and state lotteries. No wonder the young people are confused about what mother and dad really do believe" (*See You at the Top*, p. 304). It is an all-pervasive type of philosophy, even entering political and religious arenas. But the subconscious mind will not accept the reality of something for nothing.

I get some strange calls sometimes from people who think I might want to hear about a "ground floor" business. One fellow called me from Florida and said, "I'm introducing a new program into this area. I called you because you're a sharp businessman and would probably be interested."

Oh, oh, I thought, *here it comes.*

"Tell me more about it," I said, curious about this scheme. I had a difficult time not laughing into the phone when he replied to my question of "What do you sell?" with the answer, "Well, we've got a trap."

I said, "I know that, but what are you selling?" Frankly, I was amazed that he would blatantly expose his scam at the beginning.

"Well, you see, we're selling a trap."

"I know that, but what's the product?" I couldn't believe it.

I've heard about building a better mousetrap, but I wasn't sure the market would be very big. We keep cats on the ranch.

But my intrepid caller persisted. "It's one of those traps under the sink. Best that was ever made. Man, this thing will last a lifetime. You just snap it out, clean it, and snap it back in again. No problem."

"That's really exciting," I said in my best flat tone. "What are you going to sell the customer next month?"

"Well," he fumbled, "the company is working on a lot of new

products. Look, all you have to do is sign up and let the money come in.''

He was promising the old something for nothing philosophy; he assured me that I wouldn't have to sell anything. All I had to do was use my existing business associates to do the work and I could just collect the profits.

I'd had it. I said, ''If what you've got is so good, why don't you just go and build your business? But don't try to reach into other people's businesses to recruit.''

Funny thing, I never heard another word about that company in our area. That modern-day carpetbagger must have moved on to other fields or fallen by the wayside.

Everywhere the philosophy infiltrates. A young woman was told by the personnel officer of a company, ''Why don't you come to work for a few weeks? Then I'll see that you are laid off and you can collect unemployment compensation.''

In the political arena we are promised extra service at no additional cost if we vote the right way.

Television advertising promises a lifetime of satisfying social experiences for the price of a tube of toothpaste.

Second Foundation Stone of Giving

It's been said that there are three kinds of givers: the flint, the sponge, and the honeycomb. To get anything out of the flint you must hammer it; then you receive chips and sparks. To get water out of a sponge you must squeeze it, and the more pressure you use, the more you will get. But the honeycomb just overflows with its own sweetness.

We can all be like the honeycomb, because every one of us has something to give.

The second foundation of the principle of giving is just that: We always have something to give.

There is no such thing as poor me or poor you. If we live in a universe in which one of the principles is give and you receive, and the underlying foundation stone is that there is no such thing as something for nothing, then it logically follows that we have to have something to give in order to receive. Consequently, it has to be true that we always have something to give, or it's an unfair, unjust universe.

You may be thinking, *Well, it must be unfair then because I don't have anything to give! I don't have any great talents or abilities. I can't speak. I don't have much money. I'm just a housewife. I'm just an electrician. I'm just a plumber. I'm just a student. I'm just an old retired reject.* Wait a minute! You're not "just" anything. You are a beautiful, unique, wonderful creation of God himself, endowed with all the talent and ability to do anything you set your mind to do! You always have something to give.

What can we give out of our storehouse of talents? We all have different gifts: Some can paint, or sing, or write; others have naturally endowed skills in building, working with our hands, or understanding mathematics. However, there is one thing we all can give: Everyone can give a word of praise. You and I as humans on planet earth thrive on praise. We are built up by praise and destroyed by criticism. The writer of Proverbs says, "Kind words are like honey—enjoyable and healthful" (Proverbs 16:24, TLB). Constructive criticism is an attitude that may be as destructive as blatant faultfinding. The person who chirps, "Now I only mean to help," may be more of a bird of prey than a person of prayer.

Whatever you give, you will receive. If you give praise, you will receive praise that builds you up. When you give criticism you are in the process of destroying yourself.

The mother said, "Keith, you are such a help to me. I don't know how I could manage the grocery shopping without you." So Keith responds with behavior that reflects the words of praise.

If Mother says, "Keith, you're a lousy helper. My back is breaking from carrying all the groceries." Keith takes that criticism and the next time he has the opportunity, passes it on to his little sister: "You're no good at all. Why can't you help me clean up the living room?"

The Ninety-Day Challenge

Whenever I suggest the ninety-day challenge at a seminar the reactions are volatile. The challenge is this: for the next ninety days, totally eliminate all criticism of your spouse. If you're not married, take the same challenge and apply it to the person with whom it is most difficult for you to get along. Maybe it's a brother or sister, mother or father; perhaps it's the employer who makes your daily life ulcerville. Whoever it is, for a period of three months, not only eliminate the criticism, but also look for the good and give a word of praise.

Once after I voiced this challenge in a church conference, a little gal came charging down the aisle, heading straight for me. I hoped that she would stop before she crashed into the altar rail. She was about five rows from the front when she shook her finger at me and shouted, "Look here, Mr. Ross, if I did what you said I wouldn't be able to talk to him."

She was serious. "Whoa! Wait a minute. There must be something good about your husband or you wouldn't have married him in the first place," I said. This was not what I would call a theologically profound statement, but she changed from belligerence to thoughtfulness and answered, "Well, I guess that must be true."

Another time a couple told me, "Skip, we just wanted you to know that we appreciated your seminar and decided to accept your ninety-day challenge."

"That's great," I smiled. "I'm always pleased when people give it a try."

"One thing you ought to know," the husband said sheepishly, "we accepted that challenge just an hour and a half ago, but we've started over four times already!"

They were anticipating my amused reaction. "As long as you are willing to start over, we're in good shape. It's when you don't want to begin again that we have real problems with the whole process."

A woman came to me with her mouth set in a rigid line and said, "Look, I won't criticize my husband, but could I just think it?"

No, I'm sorry, that won't work. Thinking criticism is the same as verbalizing, sometimes worse, because you harbor the resentment and it festers.

One man wanted to create his own rules. "Skip, could I save it up for ninety days and then let her have it on the ninety-first?" No.

Totally eliminate all criticism for ninety days.

Another friend of mine painted this picture of his home life: "I arrive home at 6:15 and dinner is supposed to be ready, because I have to leave at 6:45 to drive for an hour to a meeting. I've worked hard at the office all day, up at 5 A.M., rode the subway to work, rode the subway home at night. There I am, with just a few minutes to grab a bite and change my clothes. I'm standing there in the kitchen and not only is dinner not ready, it's not started. Do you mean to say I can't say anything to her?"

That's right! No criticism.

Look for the good. Give a word of praise. It will change your life. What if you go for thirty-six days and blow it? Start back to day one. Accept the challenge for ninety consecutive days.

One couple decided to accept the challenge and five days after they began their little six-year-old boy said, "Mommy, what happened to Daddy?" She said, "Why? What do you mean?"

"I don't know," said the child. "He's just different."

She told him about the ninety-day challenge and the little boy got excited and went to tell all of his brothers and sisters what Mom and Dad were doing. They all decided to refrain from any criticism for ninety days. They sent me a letter saying that the family was together for the first time in years.

One of our young Circle A campers wrote us: "If you don't remember me, I'm the one who hurt her arm. I wanted to write to tell you that we got my arm X-rayed here, and they said it was doing better. I don't have my cast off yet. One of my dreams already came true. I got a skateboard. And about the challenge to be nice to one person in your family . . . I chose two because I couldn't make up my mind. I already had to start over once."

Give the word of praise for ninety consecutive days, and it will change your life. What you give you will receive, and in the process of receiving praise you will be encouraged and become a better person.

Third Foundation Stone of Giving

The final element in our foundation is this: You always give with the expectation of receiving. Today there are some dangerous concepts which are voiced by people who would lead you to believe that if you give you will get. You say, "Well, that's what you just said, isn't it?" No. The popular philosophy is diametrically different from giving and receiving as I understand it. The give and get people teach that you give specific things to people to gain certain results from that person. It is power manipulation of lives. It's a calculated effort to take care of number one. It may work for a short time. However, it is a greedy, selfish philosophy and can only harm the participants.

The principle of giving is that you give and give, over and over again, not knowing when it will come back to you or how, but expecting that ultimately you will receive. Be open to receive when it comes.

Many people are very talented at giving, but have not mastered the art of receiving. I struggled with this for years as a boy, as a teenager, and then as a college student. I watched the lives of church people who gave so much of themselves, always being available on the front lines of serving, but were unwilling to allow others to give to them.

Many of us are guilty of this: Someone comes up and says, "That's a nice dress." With slightly downcast eyes you say, "It's three years old." They didn't ask you its age; they complimented you on your appearance. "That was a marvelous talk you gave." You answer, "If they'd given me more notice, I could have done a lot better."

When we are unwilling to receive even simple compliments, we short circuit the principle of giving and receiving. Accept a compliment gracefully, with thanksgiving, and allow it to flow through you and give it away again. It's a marvelous experience of life to try to give it away faster than it comes back.

A letter came from a friend who wrote this:

"In your seminar, you mention several laws—one in particular, the law of giving. The law works. I have had several occasions to utilize this law. The most dramatic happened just the other day.

"Several weeks ago, the president of our company made an announcement that there will be no raises given this year due to the economic situation. Previous to this company-wide meeting, I had decided to give money to the United Way, an organization I feel strongly about. Although I was one of the low men on the totem-pole in terms of pay, I ended up pledging twice as much as anyone, even those who make five times what I make!

"Somebody asked me how I could afford to give away so much. I told them I could not afford not to give away money. I explained to them the law of giving or sowing and reaping.

"Anyway, the other day, I had my employee evaluation and would you believe . . . they gave me a raise! I was the only person to get one in a year.

"Well, Skip, some may say that my raise was just a coincidence. Could be. But I believe the principle works."

The principle works powerfully in every area of life. It is not designed to be a bribe for God to give back to you. As I see it, the principle of giving begins to develop a storehouse from which we give in greater abundance. As we give, in return we receive more, which increases the storehouse from which we give.

"It is possible to give away and become richer! It is also possi-ble to hold on too tightly and lose everything. Yes, the liberal man shall be rich! By watering others, he waters himself" (Proverbs 11:24, 25, TLB).

GIVING AND RECEIVING

I launched a smile; far out it sailed
On life's wide troubled sea.
And many more than I could count
Came sailing back to me.

I clasped a hand while whispering,
"The clouds will melt away."
I felt my life was very blessed
All through the hours that day.

I sent a thought of happiness
Where it was needed sore,
And very soon thereafter, found
Joy adding to my store.

I wisely shared my slender hoard,
Toil-earned coins of gold;
But presently it flowed right back.
Increased a hundredfold.

I helped another climb a hill,
A little thing to do:
And yet it brought a rich reward,
A friendship that was new.

I think each morning when I rise,
Of how I may achieve,
I know by serving I advance,
By giving I receive.

Thomas Gaines

5

YOU GUARD THE DOOR

Principle #2: The Principle of Exclusion
*"Get rid of what you don't want to make room for what you
want."*

When I was first exposed to the concept of getting rid of what
you don't want to make room for what you want, I thought it was
crazy. Some of the husbands who find their wives putting this
principle into action in their wardrobes may dress me in unflatter-
ing tar and feathers. But listen a minute.

I was told several years ago to go home and throw out everything in my clothes closet that I hadn't worn in a year. The precept
was that as long as it hangs in your closet it is a negative drain upon
your energy, your attitude, and hampers the possibility of getting
new clothes. When I heard this I thought, *Dumb*. At that point in
my life I didn't have a lot of clothes, and I couldn't afford to buy
anything new. However, I decided to take the challenge anyhow
and began to go through my closet, thinking there might be a shirt
or two, perhaps a tie. Before I was finished I pulled out four boxes
of clothes. Some of them I hadn't worn for four or five years.

My hands lingered over my favorite sport coat. How could I part
with it? It had been a very expensive coat, the sort of thing I felt
rich in every time I wore it. Sure, it was out of style, the collar was

frayed, and the elbows were pretty thin. But I was emotionally attached to that coat. The feelings of being wealthy, looking good, of being attractive to other people, were tied into wearing that coat. If I got rid of the coat, then, I thought, I wouldn't experience those pleasant emotions any more. I mustered my courage and stuffed that coat into the Salvation Army box.

Emotionally we are attached to attitudes more strongly than we are to material possessions. We have built up habitual patterns of thought about many things. These habit patterns have become our attitudes. We have attitudes about ourselves, about other people, relationships, parents, and children. Some of these attitudes are so negative they will ruin lives, careers, and marriages. Once established in the mind, these attitudes tend to reinforce themselves by attracting similar thoughts.

Norbert Wiener, an MIT professor of mathematics, was one of the real pioneers in the field of study known as Cybernetics. In 1947 he published a book called *Cybernetics*, in which he hypothesized that negative thoughts have the ability, neurologically, to attract to them similar thoughts. Bringing this idea together with modern brain research, we have a physiological explanation of how it works.

"Professor Roger Sperry of the California Institute of Technology has conclusively proven that individual neurons (cells in the brain) develop the ability to recognize one another by acquiring 'individual identification tags, molecular in nature.' . . . Neurons, then, carrying repetitive thought patterns have the power—through transfer of 'identification tags' to involve more and more neurons in their habitual activity" (*Psychofeedback*, p. 76).

In other words, negative attracts negative, positive attracts positive.

Negative People Are Expensive

In this battlefield of life one of the first places I began to wage war was against the negatives of people association. Except for yourself, your spouse, or your children, you need to move away from the negative people whose attitudes will tear you down. A businessman said to me, "You just don't understand. My job requires me to be around negative people." True, there are many jobs which are in an atmosphere that breeds negativism. It may sound harsh, but if you can't handle it and you carry these attitudes home, then you may need to leave the job you have.

A fellow at one of my seminars listened to what I said and a couple of weeks later said he had made a decision. "I decided to sell my whole business," he said, "and dissolve the partnership. It's going to cost me thousands of dollars, but there has been such a negative input from my partner that I can't afford to be in that position any longer."

That's a drastic move. However, the people who associate with happy, excited, positive people become better individuals themselves. Someone said, "A man is known by the company he avoids."

I used to avoid people who were successful. Somehow I thought they wouldn't have time or interest in me. However, as my life began to change and as I moved more and more in the circles of those people who were achievers, I discovered they were more willing to talk and share than anyone else. That's one of the reasons why they got where they were. People who are successful are where they are, for the most part, because they care about people. They are willing to spend time with them.

When I began to apply the principles of exclusion in my life there were certain friends who would answer the simple question of "How are you doing?" with a long recital of their illnesses or bad fortune. My stomach would begin to churn, my attitude would plummet. Finally, I gulped and decided to take charge. One day I said, "Look, I love you guys and appreciate you, but one of three things is going to happen. Either you're going to come to my experience of life or I'm going to come to your experience of life, or we're going to part company. Those are the only three choices we have." As the shock value began to be realized, I continued. "I respect you and would love to spend time with you, but I'm telling you right now that I'm not coming to your negative experience of life. It appears obvious from the fact that you will not say anything positive, that you are not where I'm going, so even though I love you, I've got to say good-by."

Jesus told his disciples if the people in a city or village didn't receive them or listen to the Good News, to shake the dust from their feet and move on.

Someone once said to me, "Find the most highly successful persons in your community, make an appointment and take them out to dinner. Ask them how they got where they are, quiz them about their motivation and methods."

That was one of the best pieces of advice I've ever had. It cost me a lot on meals when I couldn't afford it, but I discovered in later years that the investment returned many times.

George Washington is quoted as saying, "Associate yourself with men of good quality if you esteem your own reputation; for 'tis better to be alone than in bad company."

You and I cannot afford negative people in our lives.

Watch What You Watch

The second area where we need to wage war is in the realm of what we watch. I don't intend to lecture on the evils of television, for it is one of the most important means of communication in our time.

Television can create fears in children without parents realizing it. A researcher at Children's Television Workshop wrote in the January 10, 1981, issue of *TV Guide,* "For one thing, children can look completely delighted when they're actually frightened by something they're watching on TV. They lean forward, stare catatonically, become completely lost in the experience." Only later, when the child can't sleep and screams in the night do parents discover what their youngster was really feeling. Television speaks to us on an emotional level, influencing our lives for better or worse.

No one can watch a program that portrays the sordid details of three-way love affairs, illegitimacy, abortion, and perversion without being affected. One newspaper, either in a serious effort to recap the soap opera plots or in jest at some of the involved situations, listed what had happened on certain programs the previous week. Try this for positive mind-filling: ''Susan made a drunken fool of herself by storming into a board meeting and accusing Jim of harassing her because he allowed his own alcoholic wife to die. Jim couldn't deny it. Don suggested Joyce go with him on his Swiss business trip but agreed to keep their engagement a secret. David insisted Beau wasn't welcome in his house or in his daughters' lives. . . .''

The scenario never quits. Meanwhile, back in the living room, the children who are home from school with a cold are watching what Mom digests each day. The child's views of marriage, romance, honesty, and emotional stability are being formed by the intricate human relationships on the tube. The habit patterns of thought are beginning which will affect the course of those lives from that point onward.

Psychologists tell me that they can take four different people, watching four separate programs: a mystery, a romance, a documentary, and a horror story. Connecting these people to electrodes, they test their saliva and perspiration, and from a test room removed from where the individuals are watching, tell which person is watching which show. They can switch channels and the person monitoring from the testing room will say, ''You just changed channels. Person *A* is watching the romance, person *B* is now looking at the horror story, and so on.'' Without fail they are able to tell which person is watching which program. Reactions are determined by what we see on the screen.

Also, television commercials are designed to move us in certain directions. Some, of course, urge us to buy the product or service offered by the advertiser. However, there are some people who have a certain philosophy of life and attempt to make us believe their way.

In his book, *Subliminal Seduction,* Wilson Bryan Key explains, ''The basis of modern media effectiveness is a language within a language—one that communicates to each of us at a level beneath our conscious awareness, one that reaches into the uncharted mechanism of the human unconscious. This is a language based upon the human ability to subliminally or subconsciously or unconsciously perceive information" (p. 11).

Some time ago there was a commercial which ran for a period of time. They don't show it any more because somebody found out what it was, and it was taken off the air. It was a commercial advertising fried chicken. Innocent enough, wouldn't you say? In this commercial an astronaut was seen taking a space walk. What does that have to do with fried chicken? Who knows? Anyhow, the astronaut was bouncing through space, with the huge space capsule marked with those beautiful letters USA. Suddenly, his life-support system hose breaks; the music changes. The camera closes in on the astronaut as he frantically searches for his life-support hose. You'll never believe who has an extra hose. Right, it's the chicken who comes to the astronaut with the life-saving air. Catch the drama now. The camera zooms in and as the spaceman grabs for the chicken to save his life, the U and A of USA are blocked out and the only letter you see on the side of the capsule is an S. Then the life-support connection begins to whip around wildly, as we have seen objects do on the sides of space capsules in televised viewings. As it lashes around it flips to form an E and then again to form an X. In the conscious mind, very few would see it, but the subconscious mind discerns: S-E-X.

I know this sounds far-fetched. What does fried chicken have to do with sex? I don't know. However, if somehow that brand of chicken can be attached to one of the deepest emotional and physical experiences of life, you will be more likely to buy that brand of fried chicken than some other type.

In his book *Media Exploitation* (pp. 14, 15), the author says, "It is not at all improbable that under intensive, repetitive and long-term subliminal bombardment, entire value systems could be rearranged."

Considering the fried chicken commercial, hear what Key has to say: "Since American media, through the use of subliminal embedding, has sexualized virtually everything that is advertised or presented in media, the sexualization of food is perhaps the ultimate triumph."

Subliminal advertising is a powerful tool to program your mind.

When the boys and girls come to our ranch they seldom have withdrawal pains over the lack of television. They are so busy with positive activities that the messages from the big box are swept out of their minds, for a time, at least.

Falling on Deaf Ears

We live in a time when there are many forces vying for our loyalty; voices striving for our allegiance and support are heard from many communication centers. The music we hear imprints lasting impressions upon our minds and attitudes.

Throughout history, music has played a vital part in personal lives and nations. Centuries before the birth of Christ, Plato, one of the leading philosophers of all ages, said: "Indulged in to excess, music emasculates instead of invigorating the mind, causing a relaxation of the intellectual faculties, and debasing the warrior into an effeminate slave, destitute of all nerve and energy of soul."

Old Plato may not have recognized the very positive value of music as did King David, who was a pretty fair country harpist himself. "King David also ordered the Levite leaders to organize the singers into an orchestra, and they played loudly and joyously upon psaltries, harps, and cymbals" (2 Chronicles 15:16, TLB).

It has been scientifically proven in controlled experiments that you can take a living plant, control the atmosphere, feeding and watering, and yet its growth will be determined by the music in its environment. In a room with easy listening music, it will grow; with good classical music the plant will flourish and even lean toward the source, just as it leans toward the source of light. Place the same plant in identical surroundings, but change the music to acid rock, and it will lean away from the source of the music, wither, and die.

The war lords of Satanic worship and the manipulators in the drug culture will admit that one of the basic methods by which they move people to their philosophy of life begins with rock music. Many rock musicians are involved in the occult and Eastern religions. Some are open Satan worshipers, with songs about hell and the devil.

Although there has been much written in recent years about the negative influence of rock music, the trend has not been abated. The life styles and music of most of the popular rock groups reflect a culture that's rebellious, sadistic, and sexually promiscuous.

A wise man said, "It is easier to understand a nation by listening to its music than by learning its language." A few years before the rise of Hitler a prominent Italian composer, Pietro Mascagni, is quoted as saying, "Modern music is as dangerous as cocaine." Little did he realize at that time that the two would be so closely linked. It is estimated that 90 percent of rock music is composed under the influence of drugs.

Be careful about the music you hear. After our summer sessions at camp some of the teenagers go home and have a record-breaking spree. They hear good music for two weeks and realize that they cannot afford the messages from their cherished rock albums. We continue to emphasize that the choice is an individual matter. But if you decide to listen, at least do it with full knowledge of how you are being programmed.

Music to Your Ears

What music do you hear when people talk to you, or when you talk to yourself? Many of us listen to the degrading things people say, take the negatives into our ears, plant them in our subconscious, and pull them out to reinforce our feelings of inadequacy or unworthiness. Don't listen to the discordant music from the person who says, "You can't do it." Tune out the ones who imply that you don't have talent, or ambition, or any of the attributes which are available to you when you believe in yourself. Listen to these words that fortify your self-image; hear the image-makers and turn a deaf ear to the image-breakers.

> If you hear a kind word spoken
> Of some worthy soul you know,
> It may fill his heart with sunshine

If you only tell him so.
If a deed, however humble,
Helps you on your way to go,
Find the one whose hand helped you,
Seek him out and tell him so.*

The great Babe Ruth was a man who tuned out negative voices from without and within. He was known as the home-run king, yet he struck out more times than anyone else. Though his home-run record has been surpassed, his strike-out record still holds. This didn't keep him from swinging his bat!

One day the Babe was being interviewed at the close of a game. It had been an exciting contest, because it was the final game played for the pennant drive. The game went into extra innings and the crowd was tense. Finally the opposing team scored one run. They were ahead of the Yankees as the Babe approached the plate for the fifth time.

He had struck out four times that day. As he ambled to the plate there were two men out and one man on in the bottom of the thirteenth. If he struck out, the season was over; if he got a hit and scored a run, it would be tied. If he hit a home run, the Yankees would win. There were probably thousands of fans in those stands with muscles tighter than steel bands. Then it happened—one of those great moments in sports that is never forgotten. The count stood at no balls, two strikes. Would this be his fifth strikeout? With the next pitch, the ball was hit with a loud crack and sailed right out of the park. A home run! The Yankees had won and pandemonium broke loose on the field.

The reporters rushed out and asked, "Babe, what were you thinking about?" The great Babe Ruth smiled and said, "I was thinking about the same thing I always think about . . . the only thing I ever think about. I was thinking about hitting a home run."

He concentrated on his strengths and never allowed his weaknesses to detract from what he did best.

A prestigious American university surveyed some of its most successful graduates and asked, "Do you feel that your success in

*From *Lines to Live By*, edited by Clinton Howell, Thomas Nelson, 1972.

life is due more to concentrating on your strengths, or looking at
your weaknesses and correcting them?''

Most of these people, prominent in various businesses and pro-
fessions, answered, ''We never concentrate on our weaknesses,
we only center on our strengths.''

No Ban or Burn, Just Ignore

We should be as careful of the books we read as we are of the
company we keep, and the music we hear. One quick glance in
someone's home and you can tell where his mind is by the books
he is reading.

Some people spend time reading novels, because fiction trans-
ports them out of their workaday world into another realm of time
and fantasy. Some novels are very good, but others should never
cross the threshold of your subconscious mind. Many of the books
on the best-seller list portray an image of life that is degrading. A
man came to me once and said, ''Skip, you have to read this
book.'' When I heard the title, I said, ''No, thank you, not me.''
''But it's at the top of the best-seller list, everybody's reading it.''
I said, ''I really don't care. I was told the underlying philosophy of
that book, and I refuse to put that kind of garbage into my subconscious mind.''

A friend of mine told me about taking a current best-selling
novel on her vacation trip, prepared to enjoy many hours of reading pleasure. She soon found herself dwelling on the elements of
perverted human behavior portrayed in the book and her thoughts
were consumed by them. Although there was a compelling story
theme in the book, she deliberately left it at the hotel when they
moved on and felt a pall of negativism lift from her mind. Proverbs
says, ''An unreliable messenger can cause a lot of trouble. Reli-
able communication permits progress'' (Proverbs 13:17, TLB).

We should declare war on these ''unreliable messengers'': the
printed pages of the literature we allow to enter our minds, the
negatively oriented people who tend to destroy us, the visual im-
ages of communication which surround us today, and the words or
music which seek to undermine a positive experience of life. Only

then will we grasp another vital principle toward *dynamic living.*

We need to control what goes into the subconscious mind, because it is limited in its ability to perform by the raw materials that we give it. Some would say, "Yes, but, many of these areas you're speaking of now are only make-believe and do not really affect me at all." I understand the desire to escape the necessity of a dedicated program to guard what enters the subconscious mind. However, the subconscious mind, for all practical purposes, does not know the difference between reality and make-believe. It is simply raw material which will be used to determine your experience of life.

The principle of exclusion says, "Get rid of what you don't want to make room for what you want."

6

TURN YOUR DREAMS
INTO REALITY

Principle #3: Principle of Creation
"Decide what it is that you want, define it clearly and specifically, and write it down."

> Dear God,
>   I would like these things.
>   a new bicycle
>   a number three chemistry set
>   a dog
>   a movie camera
>   a first baseman glove
>   If I can't have them all I would like to have most of them.
>   Yours truly,
>   Eric
>   P.S. I know there is no Santa Claus.*

Children are dreamers and wishers. Before their imaginations are stifled by parents, their peers, or the realities of the world, they

---

*From *Children's Letters to God* by Eric Marshall and Stuart Hample, Simon & Schuster, Inc., New York, 1966.

are able to weave magic out of the fabrics of imagination. A little boy can see himself riding on a fire engine, ready to man the hoses and climb the ladder for a rescue. A little girl can imagine herself dancing through the mansion of Daddy Warbucks, with all the servants following her.

Shakespeare said, "We are such stuff as dreams are made on," and yet many people stop dreaming because they have lost their belief in dreams coming true. Or there are those who daydream without any action.

The principle of creation is not wishful thinking or daydreaming, but what people in the field of human endeavor call "burning desire." This is the attitude which says, "I don't care what it takes, I'll do it."

This is the type of desire that Lindbergh had in 1927 when he was the first to cross the Atlantic in a single-engine plane. It's the desire that drove the boy with the weak legs and poor background to become one of the greatest track athletes of the century—Jesse Owens. It was the desire of a man to build a school to train young people to know the Bible and spread its teachings throughout the world that sprang from the ashes of the great Chicago fire of 1871—Dwight L. Moody.

The dreams that spark those burning desires can be used by those who are evil and disregard a moral, ethical structure of life. The paperhanger in Germany used these principles to convince people that they were chosen to rule as the Master Race, pure and unadulterated by imperfections or weaknesses. He could move people to do immoral acts by deciding what he wanted, defining the goals, and acting upon them. This is a powerful principle.

Give Me This Day My Own Baseball Glove

I was twelve years old when I first felt burning desire. One Sunday morning in church the superintendent of our Sunday school department announced, "The child who reads the most chapters of Scripture in the next three months will get a beautiful prize." Big deal. That didn't excite me at all. I didn't start reading, because he didn't show us the prize until the following week. When he walked into the department, he held up the object of my dreams. It was the most gorgeous baseball glove I had ever seen. I had to have it.

Understand that as the son of the pastor of that church, I was watched more closely than any other kid in the congregation. One day, for instance, a sweet grandmotherly lady came to me and said, "Do you know John Paul? He's my grandson. He goes to your school, and he says that he watches you constantly, because anything you do must be all right." I said, "Thank you very much," and gulped. People were always watching what the preacher's kid was doing. When I played shortstop on the church ball team, I was sure all eyes were upon me. I was not noted for my athletic prowess, and the ball seemed to have a way of finding its way around me. I had some very valid excuses why I missed—a blade of grass or a little rock got in my way. However, one morning I knew why I couldn't catch that elusive little missile.

The morning I saw that baseball glove as the prize, I knew I had the answer. That glove was so big, and all the fingers were tied together by a leather thong. I knew if I played short stop with that glove it would just reach out there and "suck 'em up." No ball could slip through those fingers! I had to have it.

I began to read for my life. It didn't matter what I had to do during those three months: I got up early every morning before I went to school; I left the playground at recess time and lunch time; I went off in a corner and read the Bible. Every night for three months I read. Sometimes I went to sleep with my head flopped on my Bible and the lights still on. My mother would pull the Bible from underneath my head. I must have thought I would get credit by osmosis!

When that contest was over I had read twice as many chapters of the Bible as any other kid in the class and got the glove.

In a move from Ohio to Michigan a few years ago, my wife Susan was going through some old trunks and brought out that glove. "Is this it?" she asked, holding up a small, shriveled piece of leather. It's amazing what a different perspective we have on things we wanted at one time. We decided that we were going to have the glove bronzed and save it as a reminder of that experience of burning desire.

What Is Your Burning Desire?

What do we really want? Many of us have desires, but are afraid to face them for different reasons. Some of us are afraid because we don't think we can do it. Others put a moral stigma on desires because they think the desires are wrong. Others of us do not believe we are worth the effort. Some of us are afraid because we're afraid of everything!

I have counseled with many, particularly my business associates, who completely deny the existence of any burning desire in their lives. I discovered that often this exists because it's easier to say, "There is nothing I really want," than it is to admit one has dreams and goals which we believe can never become reality. The acknowledgment that a dream exists carries with it the responsibility to try to make it happen.

If our burning desire is for an object, an accomplishment, or a skill that will benefit us, our family, or mankind, and harm no other living creature, then it can become a reality. What are we afraid to try? Some are afraid to try because they are afraid to fail. So what? Get up and try again!

We are goal-oriented creatures. We are designed to continue accomplishing. The alternative to trying again is not a pleasant experience. A person without a goal, void of dreams and desires, has entered psychological death. Henry Ward Beecher put it this way: "But if a man has come to that point where he is so 'content' that he says, 'I don't want to know any more, or do any more, or be any more,' he is in a state in which he ought to be changed into a mummy!—Of all hideous things a mummy is most hideous; and of mummies, the most hideous are those that are running about the streets and talking."

The successful person is always willing to risk failure.

Ty Cobb was one of baseball's greatest players. During his career he stole more bases than anyone else and set a record that stood for decades. However, there was another player who was a better base stealer than Ty Cobb. His name was Max Carey and one season he attempted fifty-three stolen bases and succeeded fifty-one times, an amazing 96-percent record. Ty Cobb's percentage was only 71 percent. However, the year he set the record he tried 144 times and stole 96 bases. Because he was willing to try harder and chance failure, he became one of the legendary names in baseball. Max Carey, who played it safe, is scarcely remembered.

The only way we can grow is to keep stretching our capacities. Move out of those comfort zones; do things we've never done before. Don't be afraid to feel that burning desire.

The story is told of the young man who approached the philosopher, Socrates, and said, "Socrates, teach me what you know." The great teacher looked at the young man and said, "Do you really want to know all that I know?"

"Oh, yes, teacher, I do," the student replied.

"Walk with me for a time," Socrates said. So they walked for a while in silence. The learned philosopher slipped his arm around the young man's shoulder and guided him off the path and into the shallow waters of a lake. The young man thought that was a strange way for the philosopher to teach him what he knew, but after all he was Socrates, so the student decided to go along with what was happening.

They continued to walk into the water; it rose to their ankles, then knees and hips, until finally they were standing in water to their shoulders. Suddenly the arm that was around the young man's shoulders tightened around his neck and pulled him underneath the water. This was a *very* strange way to teach the student what he wanted to know. But this was Socrates, after all, so he submitted. He grabbed a breath before he went under, so he wasn't bothered for the first fifteen or twenty seconds, but after about thirty seconds he wondered when Socrates was going to let him up. He gave him a signal to indicate that he had been under long enough and wanted to get out. Another few seconds and the young man began to fight with all he was worth. He kicked and clawed and scratched, but the hold was strong and he lost his strength. At that moment, Socrates pulled him out of the water, dragged him to the shore, and began to revive him.

When he caught his breath, angry and confused, the student looked into the face of one of the greatest philosophers of all time and said, "What was that all about?"

Socrates looked into his eyes and said, "When you want to know what I know as much as you just wanted to live, then you will know."

That kind of desire is what is known as burning desire!

Decide what it is you want. Don't decide what somebody else wants for you, it's not their responsibility. What do you want? The first step in the principle of creation is to decide what it is you want. Is it important enough to you to inspire you with a burning desire; will the "baseball glove" in your life be such a strong desire that you will work and plan how to get it?

Second Step: Principle of Creation

Vague definitions will produce vague results. After you decide what you want, define it clearly and specifically. If you want a new home, look at homes, get some blueprints, consult an interior decorator, and have a clear picture of it in your mind. If you want a new car, determine what model you want, the color, the equipment.

Why do you think the charities and missionary organizations send pictures in their appeal letters? When you look at the face of a starving child you have a clear, defined reason to give to that organization.

The power of clearly defined goals is well documented in human experience. The necessity of it can be illustrated from my own travels. I do a considerable amount of flying; I have often wondered what passengers on an airliner would do if the captain's words came over the intercom at take-off with this message:

"Good morning, ladies and gentlemen. This is Captain Jones speaking to you from the flight deck. I'd like to welcome you aboard flight 123 . . . or is it 321 . . . 231? Oh well, it doesn't really matter, since I don't know where we are going today, any-how—I just thought we'd take off and fly for a while . . . north, south, a little east. I certainly hope the weather will be okay and that we have enough fuel on board. Of course, that's a little diffi-cult to calculate, since we don't know where we are going, nor which route we are taking if we did know. As you can see, we're just going to 'fly by the seat of our pants' as they say. It should be a very casual morning, so sit back, relax, and enjoy your flight.''

I don't know about you, but I'm not flying with that guy! He doesn't have a clearly defined goal. He'll never make it. I'm getting off that plane as fast as I can.

A ridiculous story? Yes, I certainly hope so. But I suspect it would be a startling revelation if we knew how many people live their entire lives in that exact manner. You need not only to know your wants and dreams, but to specifically lay out the details of their accomplishment.

I have a good friend in Southern California who wanted a certain home. He had a fairly good business going, but the home he wanted seemed out of his reach. However, on October first of a certain year, he sent out invitations to three hundred people for a housewarming at the specific address of the house he had seen. This party was to take place on October first just one year later. He had not even talked to a real estate agent, tried to arrange financ-ing, or attempted to buy that house.

When he began to negotiate, he went to the bank for a loan and was told, ''Sorry, you don't qualify.'' He said, ''Could I write you a letter and explain why I believe I qualify for a loan?'' The banker said, ''Sure,'' so he compiled all the reasons they should loan him money, and a marvelous thing happened. He got the loan, although it took almost a year, but on October first, a year after he mailed the invitations, he had a housewarming in his new home.

What would he have done if he hadn't gotten that home? I don't know. You see, he did clearly define his goal and he reached it.

Third Step: Principle of Creation

First, decide what you want. Second, define it clearly. Third, write it down.

Does it really make any difference whether you write it down or not? Yes, it really does. I don't know everything that happens in writing, but it works. Maybe it's the focusing of your attention, maybe it's when you come to the point where you can define it clearly and specifically enough to crystallize your thinking into black and white. Perhaps it also has something to do with those neurological connections of cells in the brain.

Here's the next challenge for you: take a three-by-five-inch card and write down a list of ten things you want to happen to you in the next year. Don't figure out how they're going to happen, just write them down. Perhaps some of them will deal with the mental experience of your life, or your spiritual, business, physical, social, or family goals. Balance your list among the six major areas of your life. Whatever part of life you want to affect by this process, write down a goal in that area.

I understand the difficulty in believing this process can make a difference. I experienced a challenge in that area when I first started doing this. I said, "I am an intelligent human being, I don't need to write down my goals."

I was told, "Write them down."

"I have eight years of higher education, three degrees. I can remember my goals."

"Write them down."

"I don't believe it makes any difference."

"Write them down."

"But how does it work?"

"Write them down."

"But I . . ."

"Write them down!"

I finally figured out what he was trying to say—write down your goals.

Others must have similar problems of belief. A lady approached me after one of my recent seminars and said, "Skip, I've attended five of your seminars and it's not working for me like I thought it would."

After asking her a few questions I finally hit on the problem. "Have you taken the time to write down what it is that you want?" She said, "Well, no, I haven't. Every time you tell us to take a three-by-five card and write, I never have one with me."

Whatever you have, grab it now and write down ten things. The cards are handy because you can carry them with you, but even if you have to rip off your shirt collar, write them down! When you write down your goals in the various areas of your life, write them as if they are already realities. Eliminate such phrases as: "I'm going to," "I hope so," or "I will." Instead, say, "I am," "I have," "It is now." Use present tense.

When you have written down the ten things you want in the next year, read them every morning and every night—every morning and every night. After going over this at our youth ranch, whenever the boys and girls see me they automatically say, "Every morning, every night, every morning, every night."

At the Circle A ranch young people come from all over the country to spend two weeks with us. We run five consecutive sessions to teach the concepts of dynamic living. Every morning for two hours I share the principles with them. Then we have some recreational times and work projects. Susan and I are thrilled with some of the reports that come back to us from the young people and their parents. In fact, sometimes the kids apply the principles before they leave camp and discover that they work.

On the final day of camp we conduct a little quiz. The first part of the test pertains to what we have been talking about for two weeks. The second part the young people take time to write down ten things they want to happen in the next year. During this particular session, one boy had written down his ten items, and I told him to begin reading them right then, every morning and every night.

This little guy was on his way to the airport the next day and somehow left the ranch too late and missed his plane. Our staff people had to bring him back to the ranch. That afternoon they drove him into town to get another flight and he missed it again.

The next day he missed a third flight. On his third trip back to the ranch, he said, "Man, this stuff really works. The first thing I wrote down on my card is, 'I'm coming back to Skip's ranch.' I haven't even been gone two days and I've been back three times already!"

We have kids who are reporting A's and B's on their report cards because they began to program themselves and said, "That's what I want, that's what I have, and that's the way I am."

One man wrote me: "I have my cards and I'm reading them. I've been successful in getting our seven-year-old daughter to do the same. On her card she has written: crayola markers, gold chain with beads, diamond ring, canopy bed, skirt, gray jacket, Darci clothes, stereo, and baby clothes. As you can see I've sprouted a dreamer. She told her dubious thirteen-year-old brother, 'It really works!' She has gotten her markers and her gold chain."

Another youngster wrote down on his card that he wanted a specific tape recorder. He didn't have the money, but he described exactly which one he wanted. He knew to the penny what it would cost. Within a couple of days after leaving the ranch he received a call at home from a lady who said, "You worked for me some time ago and I never paid you. If you'll come over I'll give you the fifteen dollars you have coming." The next day another neighbor called with the same message! A few days later someone called and said, "I have a job I'd like you to do. If you come over I'll pay you ten dollars." All of a sudden he had almost enough to buy the tape recorder. He was reading his card every morning and every night when his parents went on a trip and walked into a store where they saw the exact tape recorder he wanted on sale for the amount of money he had received in a matter of ten days after he wrote it on his card!

Right now I challenge you to write down ten things you would like to happen to you in the next year. Don't worry about how they are going to happen. Don't try to figure it out. Just write them down and read your list every morning and every night and you will discover that it will happen for you as it happens for others. We debated about putting a space right here in the book for you to write your goals. But they are so handy on a three-by-five-inch card, get one and do it now!

While you are making your list and putting it on cards, here are a few seed thoughts to think about throughout the day:

If you want your dreams to come true, don't oversleep.

God desires us to soar like eagles, but many are content to scratch like sparrows.

If you are satisfied just to get by, step aside for the man who isn't.

"Hope deferred makes the heart sick; but when dreams come true at last, there is life and joy" (Proverbs 13:12, TLB).

THE ARTIST WITHIN US

Principle #4: Principle of Visualization
"Get a clear mental picture of what you want, infuse it with emotion, and hold onto it."

The great writers of our time are able to transport us from our living room chair to exotic lands, other eras of time, strange cultures where people live in manners which are unknown in our experience. These trips into other realms of human knowledge may enrich our lives or dirty our emotions, according to the books we choose and the authors we read. They know the power that visualization has over us.

You have the power of visualization within you to enable you to have what you want. First, get a clear mental picture of what you want, but that's not enough. To visualize the home you want to have, the trip you want to take, the child you want to adopt, may not be enough. You need to infuse it with emotion. Place yourself actively in the picture.

Susan and I were on a trip to the Bahamas and a couple who are business associates of ours went along with us. The wife was so excited about the trip because it was the first time in her life she had been farther than a few hundred miles away from her home.

When we announced that our next business trip would be to Hawaii, this woman decided she wanted to go. She began to get a mental picture and filled it with emotion. This was the way she did it. The group was leaving on the Hawaii trip the day after Christmas. She pictured the family on Christmas morning, with the kids running down the stairs to open the packages. Kids can get very excited about presents, but luggage doesn't happen to be one of them. However, in this mother's mind's eye the picture developed of her children rushing for the largest package under the tree, ripping off the wrapping, only to reveal a suitcase. Fallen faces! However, as she continued to watch them open the suitcase and look inside, there was a note that said, "Pack as fast as you can. We leave in sixteen hours for Hawaii."

That was visualizing with emotion! From there she pictured her husband, herself, and their three children flying across the Pacific, landing in Hawaii, and then standing in the surf at Waikiki, with the soft, fragrant breezes of the Pacific blowing their hair. They watched the sunset as it dropped behind Diamond Head.

By the way, they went with us to Hawaii and had a marvelous time!

Einstein said, "Imagination is more important than knowledge." And Napoleon believed, "The human race is governed by its imagination." "Imagination disposes of everything; it creates beauty, justice, and happiness, which is everything in this world" (Pascal).

There is a tremendous power in imagination. We are very creative people, and yet most of us have stifled that creative ability.

Unleash Your Creativity

A survey was done to discover the creativity level of individuals at various ages. After all the testing, the statistics indicated that 2 percent of the men and women who were in their forties were highly creative. As they looked at younger people, the results emerged that 2 percent of the thirty-five-year-olds were highly creative; 2 percent of the thirty-year-olds were highly creative. This went on down to each age group until they reached the seven-year-old children. Ten percent of them were highly creative. However, further study showed that 90 percent of the five-year-olds were highly creative. Between the ages of five and seven, 80 percent of us who are highly creative develop an image, a picture, an attitude that we are not creative, and we begin to deny that particular part of our God-given equipment.

I want you to know that our creative ability, our imagination, is tremendously important when we talk about the principle of visualization.

What is the power of our visualizing abilities? We are more capable, have more talent and ability than we think we have. It's inside of us right now just waiting for the channel to burst through.

A man called a real estate agent one day and said, "I'm really tired of the place where I'm living. I'd like you to come out and list my home." The agent came out and the man gave him a description of the home of his dreams. He listed the number of rooms he wanted, the acreage upon which the home would nestle, the amount of space he wanted in the rooms, and the type of architecture.

The agent took down all the specifications and left. A few days later his client called him and shouted into the phone, "I'm so excited! I found exactly the house I've been looking for."

"Tell me about it," the agent said to his client.

"I'll read you the description," the man said. "It's right here in the paper." With that he read the description of the house with the number of rooms he wanted, the acreage, the amount of space, and every detail. "It's got everything I've always wanted," he said.

"Excuse me, sir," said the realtor. "Are you playing a joke on me?"

"Of course not, I'm reading about the home of my dreams. Can you find this house?"

The realtor said, "Certainly I can find it. I listed it."

The buyer asked the agent to come over right away and take him to see this special property. When the agent arrived he said, "Come on, I'm ready. Let's go."

The realtor looked at his client, and seeing that he was serious, replied, "We don't have to go anyplace. The ad you read was the one I wrote about your house. You are living in the home of your dreams right now.''

We are just like that amazed man. So many times we doubt our abilities and potential, particularly in the area of creative imagination. If somehow we could see objectively who we are, we'd understand what great talent is already within us. We have within us the creative ability to visualize what we want. We don't have to search for that ability outside of ourselves.

Practice in Your Imagination

One of the really exciting discoveries of current brain research and human motivational studies has shown that for practical purposes an imagined, visualized experience is almost the same as the real thing.

Some high school basketball teams were tested for their free-throw shooting ability. However, before the testing program began the testers instructed the members of the teams to shoot free throws and then the percentages were recorded. How many free throws out of 100 could they score?

Then two teams were sent onto the basketball floor for five hours a day for two weeks and told, ''What we want you to do is for each of you to practice every day shooting free throws and improve on the percentage of shots you score out of 100.'' All of those fellows practiced for five hours a day, every day for two weeks.

Two teams served as the control in the experiment. They could not touch a basketball for two weeks.

Two other teams were told, ''Spend a couple of hours a day shooting baskets and the rest of the time just imagining that you are shooting baskets.'' So these fellows practiced for a while and then sat down and practiced shooting baskets in their imagination.

The final test group of two teams was told to do nothing except practice over and over in their imagination. But they were told how to visualize and emotionalize the process. They were instructed to imagine that they were standing at the free throw line. The ball game is over. The final buzzer has sounded. The score is not in your favor, but you were fouled at the buzzer. Your team trails by one point. You have two free throws coming. If you make them both, your team wins, you are the champions of the league and go on to the playoffs. Feel yourself as you come to the line; you get the ball from the referee, you bounce the ball on the floor, trying to calm yourself down. As you get set, you feel the release of the ball as you shoot and watch the perfect arch as it swishes through the net. The crowd explodes; the game is tied. You have one more free throw coming. There's a feeling in the pit of your stomach; you are so excited you can hardly contain yourself. With the next throw, the ball goes swish through the net. You've won. The cheers are deafening. The crowd rushes down on the floor and you're hoisted on to some burly shoulders. You're the hero! You've won the championship!

For two weeks those boys practiced in their imaginations. At the end of that period the teams were tested for their free throw shooting abilities. It was discovered that the teams that were on the basketball floor shooting baskets five hours a day, fourteen days in a row, increased their percentages by about 1 percent. The teams that were told to practice a couple of hours a day and imagine shooting baskets the remainder of the time increased their percentages about 1 percent.

However, the teams that infused their imaginations with emotion, and held on to those feelings, increased their free throw shooting percentage 4½ percent!

The principle of visualization, infused with emotion, works.

On a Clear or Cloudy Day the Vision Is Great

Those who see the invisible can do the impossible. When the invisible goals are visualized and injected with enthusiasm, emotion, and specific descriptions, the power of the principle of visualization is displayed.

A friend of mine who is a writer says she visualizes her book prominently displayed in the window of a bookstore, the eye-catching cover attracting the attention of the people passing by. On the book she sees her name at the bottom, announcing that she is the author. She imagines the thrill of opening a letter which says, "Thank you for what you said. Your book meant so much to me."

When challenges face us, as they do every day, to be able to visualize where we are going, what it is we want, will give us one more method of motivation to carry us forward.

In his book, *Release Your Brakes,* James Neuman relates the story of Bill, a young infantryman who was severely injured in the Korean war. For weeks Bill was paralyzed and lay in his hospital bed, unable to move any muscles except his eyes and jaw. If he wanted to read, the nurse would put a book on a rack over his bed. After a while, Bill had an idea. He had always wanted to learn to type, so he asked for a typing textbook and began to memorize the positions of each letter on the typewriter keyboard. In his imagination he visualized his fingers touching the proper keys and the words appearing on paper. In that hospital bed he practiced typing for fifteen or twenty minutes each day, without moving a muscle.

After extensive physical therapy, Bill was able to move his hands and arms. Finally, he went into the hospital office and asked if he could use a typewriter for a few minutes. He put a sheet of paper into the machine and began to type. In his very first attempt to use his new touch-typing skill he typed fifty-five words a minute, with no errors. You see, in his visualizing, he hadn't been practicing any mistakes!

Visualization is not the same as the spiritual realm of visions. However, they may be very closely related in some circumstances, when the desires of the heart are specifically defined and the object so clearly visualized that a person is able to focus on that achievement. For instance, the famous Dutch woman, Corrie ten Boom, while a prisoner in Ravensbruck, talked with her sister, Betsie, about a home they wanted after the war. They visualized a beautiful place with a garden, and large, gracious rooms where the people wounded in body and spirit could recover from the ravages of war. They even described a staircase with a polished wood bannister, inlaid wood floors, and tall windows that flooded the rooms with light.

Not long after Corrie was released from prison camp she was

offered the use of a large house in one of the most beautiful towns in Holland. It was just as she had visualized it would look.

Emotion in a Picture

If there is something you want, cut out pictures and put them on your refrigerator, the bedroom mirror, or your dashboard. Many people do that, and yet never capture the power of the principle of visualization because they neglect that important ingredient of emotion. After I spoke about this on one occasion, a woman told me she decided to put real feeling into visualizing. In our business we have an incentive called the "yacht program." When people reach a certain level of achievement, the company sends them, all expenses paid, on a beautiful ocean-going yacht. This woman really wanted to earn the right to go on that trip. So she put a picture of the yacht on her refrigerator, another one on the bathroom mirror. She plastered pictures all over the house so she would see them everywhere she went. Then she began to visualize herself on a trip with her husband. Romance was revived, they sat on deck under a big Caribbean moon and enjoyed the warmth of the tropical breezes. She could see the clothes she wanted to wear, the food she wanted to eat. She had the principle of visualization well in hand.

"But Skip," she explained after describing her dream, "I had to stop visualizing the yacht trip."

"Why would you do that?" I asked.

"Because I would look at the pictures and put emotion into visualization, just as you said, but I was beginning to get seasick while I was doing my housework!"

Frank, a good friend and business associate, put a picture of a red Maserati on his bulletin board, and said that when he made a certain goal in the business that was the car he was going to have. The clipping came from *Road and Track,* a sports car magazine, and Frank looked at it every day. He visualized himself getting into that car and driving it down the street, feeling like a million. When he reached his new award level, he ordered the car; however, when it arrived it was the wrong color. After working hard for the exact car, he wanted it to fill his specifications.

The dealer told him he did have a Maserati in the showroom that was the color Frank wanted, but it had 1,000 miles on it. He was promised the same warranty. After considerable discussion Frank agreed to look at the car. It was gorgeous. He decided to take it home. He then found out that this was *exactly the same car* that the magazine had used in the photograph he had cut out and displayed on his dream board months earlier.

The principle of visualization is this: Get a clear mental picture (a red Maserati!) of what you want, infuse it with emotion (feel yourself driving it, Frank), and hold onto it (even when the wrong color is delivered to you).

An inventor sees his invention before all the parts are in place.

The actor visualizes the stage before the scenery is made.

The architect sketches the building in his mind before he touches the drafting table.

The student sees his name on the Honor Society roll as he struggles through studying for finals.

Jack Nicklaus, one of the leading money-winners on the professional golf circuit, said that before every shot he visualizes it in his mind's eye. He sees himself addressing the ball, the position of his feet and his head, the back swing, the club head meeting the ball. . . . His head is down, then he looks up and watches the projectory of the ball. The ball hits the green, rolls toward the cup, in line for the next shot. Nicklaus visualizes every shot in that manner. Maybe it's only a coincidence that he's one of the leading money-winners on the professional golf circuit; or maybe it's because the principle of visualization really works.

Will these principles work for you? The only ideas that will work for you are the ones you put to work.

Without a vision a nation will perish, a worthy goal will wither, a creative child of God will be defeated.

Get a clear mental picture of what you want, infuse it with emotion, and hold onto it.

SPEAK IT INTO EXISTENCE

Principle #5: Principle of Command
"Thou shalt also decree a thing, and it shall be established unto thee" (Job 22:28, KJV).

As I sit in my study to write these words I look across acres of corn ready for harvest. The abundance of grain in those fields is a natural physical illustration of the power of words. Once the corn is in the ground the process has begun which will ultimately end in harvest. We also harvest the words we plant. Someone has said, "Words once spoke can never be recalled." When we speak of the process which makes words become reality, we are dealing with a course of action that not only has a certain outcome, but also is tremendously powerful in its ability to affect our lives.

Words are strong people-movers. Emerson said, "Speech is power: speech is to persuade, to convert, to compel." There are several volumes in my library which record memorable words uttered by men and women down through the years. Many times we remember people because of what they said. Look at a few:

"We have nothing to fear but fear itself."
"Give me liberty or give me death."

"Ask not what your country can do for you, but what you
  can do for your country."
"I have a dream."
"Never in the field of human conflict was so much owed by
  so many to so few."
"Keep your face to the sunshine and you cannot see the shadow."
"The world will little note, nor long remember what we say
  here, but it can never forget what they did here."
"I am the light of the world. He that followeth me shall
  not walk in darkness."

How did you do? Did you recognize Roosevelt, Patrick Henry, John Kennedy, Martin Luther King, Winston Churchill, Helen Keller, Abraham Lincoln, Jesus of Nazareth? Of course there is a persuasive power in words that has and will continue to change the course of history. However, that is not our primary concern when we give the principle of command.

This chapter began with the summary statement taken from the book of Job in the Old Testament: "Thou shalt decree a thing, and it shall be established unto thee." Chances are King James is not reading this, so let me give you an updated translation (it might even be called the Ross translation): "Whatever you speak out of your mouth will happen, so watch out what you say!" We're talking about *your words*. You don't have to be a world-renowned orator to participate. We are referring to a process that can release life-changing power in either a positive or a negative direction.

Seneca once said, "Speech is the index of the mind." Jesus put it this way, "Out of the abundance of the heart the mouth speaks." Whatever you begin focusing on is what you speak. The spoken words reinforce the image in your mind and ultimately that mental picture may become reality.

In all six major areas of life we speak into existence problems we don't want. The power of the words we say can make the situations we desire or the circumstances we want to avoid come true.

As a youngster I became very good at speaking sickness into existence. I didn't understand what I was doing in those days, but the results were what I wanted. If I didn't want to go to school the next day I found some way not to go. The night before I'd look very listless, droop my shoulders, and say, "Mom, I don't feel well. My stomach hurts and I think I have a temperature . . . my head aches, too. I know I'm comin' down with the flu or somethin'."

By the next morning I had the signs of illness. Eventually I got so good at this ruse that I could throw up on command.

Have you ever heard someone say, "I just can't lose weight. I've tried every diet that ever came along, but I don't lose, I gain"?

Let's ask the important question, "Is that what you want?"

"Of course it's not what I want," will be the indignant reply.

Then why say it? The power of your words can speak it into existence and make it true.

Verbalize Your Future

My father was an extremely intelligent man, not well-educated, but brilliant. He understood the persuasive ability of words. He began preaching when he was fourteen and continued until just a few years before he died. There are literally thousands of people across our country today who have been changed for the better because his communication reached out and touched their lives.

But I suspect that my father was like many of us who forget, at times, the power of our words for our own future. My father never had a lot of money or made a lot of money. After he retired from the ministry he filled his hours with the complexities of the stock market. He was good. One week I watched him call several stock transactions that earned one of his friends a quarter of a million dollars in five days. However, father never acted on his own recommendation. "Why, Dad? You could have made your retirement years a lot easier financially in those five days. Why didn't you invest?"

He didn't know. Then a few years later I saw him make some money in the market; in fact, he made more in the first six months of that year than he had made in any full year in his life. Within the next eight months he lost it all, borrowed thousands, lost that, and within a short time, he died.

"Why, Skip?" you say. "Why did it happen and why do you tell that story?" My father and I were very close. I loved him dearly. That story is not one of the more pleasant memories of him, but it is a *powerful* lesson. Throughout his life my dad verbalized again and again, "My greatest fear in life is that I will die a pauper." He had the talent in many areas to achieve great things, but he died penniless and in debt, exactly as he said he would.

Dr. David Stoop, in his book, *Self Talk,* gives us another illustration. "I talked recently with a very successful businessman. He had started a new business and worked hard. The result of his work was solid growth, a good management team, and unlimited potential in the years ahead. But increasingly, the demands of the business claimed more and more of his time. Then he passed out as he was leading an important meeting. The doctors told him he had to stop all activity for three months, and then limit himself carefully for the next six months. As we talked he commented, 'Dave, I've been saying for a year that nothing can stop me, except getting sick.' He determined by his statement that the only way he could slow down was to get sick. He had set himself up. And every time he thought or said those words, he released faith in that statement. And what he believed came true" (p. 49).

Little Things Mean a Lot

I have been challenged many times whether or not the silly little things we say really make a difference. I believe it makes all the difference in the world. In fact, the unwillingness to see the power of the insignificant phrase or individual word keeps the vast majority of us from controlling our tongues and our lives!

We allow words to slip out of our mouths which are such well-worn clichés that we fail to realize their impact. For instance, "She makes me sick!" Does she really? Who makes you sick? You can make yourself sick or become ill through no fault of your own, but you can't blame anyone else.

Shakespeare said in his play, *Much Ado about Nothing,* "He hath a heart as sound as a bell, and his tongue is the clapper; for what his heart thinks his tongue speaks."

Saying that someone makes you sick or makes you angry will result in what you say. The Scriptures say that many have fallen by the edge of the sword, but not so many as have fallen by the tongue.

Whom Do You Talk To?

"I'm always late to everything."

"Every time I open my mouth I put my foot in."

"That teacher doesn't like me."

"I'm so tired I can hardly move."

"I can sell to a customer once, but they never reorder."

"I can't sit there in that draft, I'll catch my death of pneumonia."

"No one is interested in my business."

"People like that make me mad!"

Every day we are allowing words to tumble out of our mouths which are nudging the very things we don't want into existence. When I began to comprehend the strength of the spoken word and the significance of saying those things that I really did not want to happen, changes began to take place in my conversation. As I began to teach these principles it was fun to hear people stop a sentence in mid-air as they realized what they were commanding themselves to do.

A couple came to me once and said, "Skip, we've got a problem. We get discouraged in our business because we bring a new couple in as business associates and after a period of time they're on their way out, and we know we have to replace them. It just seems to happen over and over again. We know it must be us, but we don't know what we're doing wrong."

The first question I asked them was, "Who have you told about this problem?"

They looked at each other, questioning whether either one of them had discussed this with anyone else and then, almost simultaneously said, "Oh, we don't tell anybody about our business problems."

"I understand," I said, "but whom do you talk to about it?"

Maybe they thought I hadn't heard them the first time. "We don't talk to anybody. It's just a problem, you know. But you're the only one we felt we could discuss it with."

"O.K., but who do you talk to about it?"

"Skip, listen to us. We don't talk to anybody about it."

"I understand, but who do you talk to about it?"

"We don't talk to an . . ."

They got the point. "Oh, we talk to one another about it all the time."

This couple is not unusual. Husbands and wives, mothers and dads, sons and daughters, business partners, talk back and forth and speak into existence their problems. The more the problem is discussed, the more it is perpetuated.

"If I live to be 100 I will never understand women!"

"My old man just doesn't have clue one to where it's at today."

"Kids! I can't even talk to my own daughter. The generation gap is insurmountable. We don't even speak the same language."

"My boss is always on my case. Always wanting more. He's a real slave-driver."

"Boy, people sure aren't like they used to be. There isn't an employee in this place that gives a rip. We're lucky if we get one good day's work out of four."

"Bob sure doesn't understand the stress I'm under here at home. And even if he did, he probably wouldn't care."

And on and on it goes. Any of it sound familiar? What are you saying?

The couple in our previous illustration, I'm happy to report, changed what they were saying to each other and went on to build a highly successful business. They began to affirm: "Our new business associates realize quick success and continue to build a solid, profitable organization."

How to Make Positive Statements of Faith

It doesn't make any difference whether you are a business or a professional person, a homemaker or a student, young or old, you may be giving yourself negative commands every day. This next story applies to the Amway business Susan and I own, but the same precepts could apply to any type of work.

A couple we'll call John and Mary are business associates of ours in New Jersey. They were in their third and final month of qualification for a significant level of achievement in our business called Direct Distributor. To reach this level it is necessary to do a certain volume of business each month. They sailed through the first two months and were down to the wire in their third month. They called me and said, "We understand you're coming to New Jersey. We need to talk to you."

I had a couple of hours between plane flights, so we arranged to meet. When they arrived their faces were smiling, but their voices were on the floor. "This is our third month of qualification. Twenty-one days are gone and there are only nine days left. Our business volume is $350, and we need almost $7,200 more."

I got their meaning very quickly. What they were really saying was, "*Help!*"

For one hour John talked, with Mary interrupting a few times with her comments. They said, "The people in our organization have worked hard for two months. We can't ask them to do any more. It's hot and a lot of people are on vacation. There's a lot of flu going around, and when it hits it really zaps you. People don't believe us like they used to. They don't show up for appointments any more."

After an hour of this I said, "Now it's my turn. I've got one hour left, so you listen."

For the next hour I gave them certain statements that were in direct contrast to what they had said to me. I boiled it all down to seven major attitudes they were verbalizing. For every phrase they used which was negative, I made one which was directly contradictory and positive.

For instance, I gave them this statement: "Today is the best day there has ever been to sponsor people into my business. There are hundreds and hundreds of people around me, waiting to hear what I have to tell them. When I talk to them they get excited and join me. They do exactly what I ask them to do and they grow and build the business. In fact, some are so excited about the business they call me to ask if they can get in before I call them.''

Mary was writing down what I said, but John frowned a bit and said, ''But that's not true. People aren't calling me.''

I told him I didn't care whether it was true or not, just write it down. Many of us have been making negative statements of faith for so long that we have been speaking into existence those things we do not want. Such as: ''I'm afraid of people.'' ''I can't speak in front of people.'' ''I just can't quit smoking.''

When I left I told John and Mary to read those positive statements of faith out loud in front of the mirror, one hour every morning and one hour every night. Then I left to catch my plane.

I didn't hear from them for the next eleven days. The month was over and I didn't know whether they had reached their goal or not. On the second day of August John called and nearly shouted over the long distance wires. ''Skip, I just had to call you and tell you those were the most important two hours we ever spent in the business. By the way, our volume ended up at $11,850.''

When we make positive statements and say them over and over again, we'll begin to believe them. When we begin to believe it, we'll begin to see it. So many people say, ''Show me, let me see it, and then I'll believe it.'' The achievers in life say, ''I'll believe it, and then I'll see it.''

The principle of faith is strongly interwoven with the principle of command, and we will talk about that in a later chapter.

I'm Sitting on Your Shoulder

I wish there were some way I could impress upon you the importance of what you are saying. It would be an eye-opening experience if we could somehow record everything you say (to yourself as well as others) for one week and then allow yourself to listen. Do you say only what you want? Even in athletic competition I have become aware. I used to say, ''That was a lousy serve, Skip. You are really clumsy. What a dumb shot.'' Now I say, ''That's okay, Ross. Now it's comin'. You're doing better.''

I'm concerned that we become aware of what we say.

Someone told me that he began to visualize a little Skip Ross sitting on his shoulder. Every time he said something he shouldn't say, or made a negative statement, the little Skip Ross would ask, "Is that what you want?" If that visual image will help you, do it.

One day a fellow called me and said, "Skip, there's a law suit against you in the state of Rhode Island."

I asked what the law suit was for and he said, "A driving accident."

"Hey, friend," I said, "I've never driven in Rhode Island."

He began to chuckle and I thought, *This is a strange trick.* But I played along with the story. My caller said, "Do you remember Harry?" Sure, I remembered Harry. He attended a seminar I did for a church group in Rhode Island. There were only about forty of us that weekend, and we had a marvelous time, sharing these concepts from a scriptural background. When we started discussing the principle of command, Harry began to come alive. At first he wasn't sure about me, but then he began to open up and understand what I was saying.

My caller continued, "Harry was driving down the highway and talking to himself as he often does." (Did you know that you spend seventy percent of your time talking to yourself?) "And he said something he shouldn't have said and he knew it. Suddenly, there you were on his shoulder saying, 'Is that what you want?' When he turned around to say, 'No,' he plowed right into the car in front of him. Can you imagine trying to explain to the highway patrol that he was driving along talking to this little guy on his shoulder?"

I never found out if the story was true or a joke, but at least my friend found it worth his money for a long distance call.

Another time after a seminar a couple of men came up to me with a business proposition. I didn't have time to listen, so I told them to write a letter.

A few days later I received a detailed explanation of this unusual proposal. Have you ever seen the little dolls that have a string you pull to make them speak? Some manufacturer had an idea for what was called an executive Teddy Bear. When you pulled his string he said, "You're a winner. Teddy knows. See you at the top."

These entrepreneurs were proposing to make a doll that would say, "Is that what you want? Then why say it?" It was also going to say, "Say yes to your potential." However, the real gimmick in the idea was that the doll was going to look like me!

I wrote them and said that I was going to decline that particular business offer. Somehow I couldn't see myself as a little doll riding around on people's shoulders. I also decided nobody else was going to pull my string.

I received a beautiful letter from a young girl who had been with us at Circle A Ranch. She explained that the kids at school make fun of her sometimes now because she looks for the good in everything. She even got in trouble with her teacher the other day for "Talking with the little Skip on my shoulder." She went on to say that none of that mattered, because she had found a better way to live. Many areas of her life reflected the change, including her grades which had gone from all D's & F's to mostly A's and B's.

But what about you? What do you talk about all the time? Honestly, undefensively, examine your patterns of speech today.

If there were some way I could convey how dynamic the words are that you speak out of your mouth, I would do it.

He who masters his words will master his works.

Say what you want. Speak it into existence. The principle of command is a life-changing concept.

9

THE GREAT ENERGY RELEASE

Principle #6: Principle of Action
"Do it now!"

Many times I am questioned about how success really comes. Someone says, "Do you mean all I have to do is decide on a course of action, set the goal, write it down, speak of it in the right way, and automatically it appears? So I just sit back and watch this grand drama unfold?"

I have already indicated the importance of creation, visualization and command, and what I am about to say should take nothing away from that emphasis. But that's not the end of the story. There comes a point in time when you must move, act, do, perform, work, labor, toil—advance. Action is the key. Shakespeare said, "Action is eloquence; the eyes of the ignorant are more learned than their ears."

The most exquisite dream in all the world will remain a dream unless someone gets into motion to make it happen. Zig Ziglar, in *See You at the Top* shares this story; "Remember, the largest locomotive in the world can be held in its tracks while standing still simply by placing a single one-inch block of wood in front of each of the eight drive wheels. The same locomotive moving at 100 miles per hour can crash through a wall of steel reinforced concrete five feet thick. That's the way you are when you're in action'' (p. 199).

We've got to believe in our dreams, but we also have to act upon them. Clement Stone said, ''I think there is something more important than believing. Action! The world is full of dreamers, there aren't enough who will move ahead and begin to take concrete steps to actualize their visions.''

One of the most difficult aspects of actualizing a goal, seeing a dream become reality, is beginning. It's the law of inertia. Getting started is the hardest thing. But, there is a lot of truth in the adage, ''Beginning is half-done.'' Start now. What is it that is waiting for your attention? Do it now! Maybe you've had the advice I've had, ''Do something, anything. Even if it's wrong, move. It's better than sitting still.'' In the sales field we face this problem at our own front door. The most difficult door for any salesperson to get through is his own.

''But what if it's the wrong move?'' you say. ''I'd better wait until I know for sure.'' Results demand action, and goal-oriented people know that action—action now—is the only way their goals are going to be achieved. People are often tempted to hold off from acting until they are completely sure of what the end result will be. In other words, they want assurance of success before they even begin. This is absolutely wrong. . . . Thomas Edison did not wait until he knew the secret of the incandescent lamp before he began his experiments. Had there been no action, Edison would never have perfected the lamp'' (*The Miracle of Motivation*, p. 236).

A popular song of today is entitled ''Tomorrow.'' Once you've heard the tune it's so easy to walk around and sing the word over and over again.

Many people live their lives ''tomorrow.'' Scarlett O'Hara made the phrase, ''I'll think about it tomorrow,'' a popular slogan.

Have you ever said:

''I'll give him a call tomorrow''? (He may not be there tomorrow.)

"I'll begin my diet tomorrow"? (Someone will probably invite you out for dinner.)

"Some day I'm going to write a book"? (The shortest writing course is described by published authors in two words: "Do it.")

"One more day won't make any difference"? (Your competitor may get the contract.)

One of the greatest energy drains is procrastination. It is a thief that steals our dreams, our ambition, and our success. As Olin Miller of *The Chicago Sun Times* put it, "If you want to make an easy job seem mighty hard, just keep putting off doing it." However, a sense of urgency, a willingness to act *now,* will release energy we never realized we had. Many of us have had the experience of doing something we knew had to be done, going through a struggle to accomplish that task, and then experiencing great exhilaration when we were finished. The energy which was released in the process of doing a job now, instead of waiting for the "perfect time," may have seemed almost supernatural at the time. "How did I do it?" we ask ourselves. In reality, it was because you did that task without putting it off that God gave you energy you never knew you had.

Because I believe so strongly in the principle of command, I refuse to use the words, "I'm sick," or "I don't feel good." Susan, however, knows when I'm not functioning as well as I might when someone asks, "How are you?" and I answer, "Feeling pretty good." One time I had to admit I was hurting real bad, but in retrospect it was better than the alternative, which could have resulted in a painful way to die.

The Day I Almost "Baled" Out

When we first began to run our summer ranch program, there were a lot of tasks that were required around the place. Some of these tasks I was not prepared for, never having lived on a farm; however, they needed to be done. One of the pieces of large farm equipment we bought was an automatic baler. This is a machine that picks up the hay, shoves it together, wraps some heavy string around it, and bumps it out the back. That, of course, is the scientific explanation of a baler from a former city boy. On our baler there is an automatic kicker. And after the hay is baled and deposited on a tray at the back, the kicker, by use of hydraulic pressure, throws the fifty- or sixty-pound bale about ten feet in the air. The bale then lands on the hay wagon behind the baler. It's so automatic that no one has to pick up the bale of hay from the field by hand.

One day we were out working in the field and the kicker didn't seem to be operating too well. I said to the head wrangler, "Why don't you drive the tractor and let me walk in back and see if I can figure out what's wrong with this thing."

I thought I saw what was wrong and signaled for him to stop. He stopped and I began to look closer; however, I made one mistake. I failed to tell him to turn off the equipment.

I crawled inside the protective cage with the kicker and began to work. The first clue I had that I was in trouble was when I heard the familiar click of that big machine. I discovered that day how fast my reactions could be. The machine was only inches away from hitting me on the head, which could have been fatal. As it was, it caught me just above the right knee. I was knocked clear out of that cage and landed flat on my back. I was dazed for a moment, so I just laid there. The strangest thing happened. It was a brilliantly beautiful sunny day, but as I gazed into that deep blue sky, right at midday, I saw some of the most gorgeous stars floating around I had ever seen in my life.

The fellow driving the tractor looked back and knew that I must be seriously injured and needed help. He ran back toward me and then realized he hadn't shut off the tractor, so he retraced his steps to turn off the motor, but stopped and started to run back to me. He didn't know which was priority at that crucial time. He told me later he was afraid to see the gory details of what had happened to me. I stood up, a little wobbly, that's certain, and said, "Brian, I'm fine. I'm just going to walk behind for a while and see if I can figure out what's wrong with this thing." I can't honestly say I really wanted to get up, endure the pain in that leg and get the hay in. But I saw that rain was on the way and I knew that bruise needed stretching. I had to do it now.

For about the next two hours I walked behind that baler, trying to keep the stiffness out of my leg. When Brian left I continued baling for another two hours until the job was done. When I returned to the house someone said, "How are you doing?" and I said, "I'm doing fine." Kim, my younger daughter, saw it was difficult for me to maneuver down our winding staircase and pressed for information about what had happened. I believe so strongly in the principle of command that saying I was fine was most of the battle won. However, the principle of action was also present, because without the accompanying action of finishing the job that day, there would have been no sense of accomplishment or release of energy. I could have allowed the hay to stay in the field and be ruined. I could have gone to bed to nurse the injury along and without a doubt have been an invalid for weeks. (The doctor later assured me I could, maybe should have been.) But I brought together three powerful friends in my life: faith, command, and action. The hay has long since been eaten by our horses and reprocessed for the fields, and I move freely on this leg to run, walk, ski, play tennis or whatever else is required.

Tired Is a State of Mind

One night I came home and broke one of my principles. I said to Susan, "Boy, I'm really tired." We were leaving on a long trip the next day and the usual preparations needed to be made. My Susan, considerate wife that she is, said, "Look, there's nothing you really have to do. Why don't you rest downstairs for a while, and I'll pack the bags; then you can go to bed early. We have to get up at 4:30 to get to the airport."

Suddenly it hit me. I knew I couldn't do that. I had a desk full of stuff waiting for me to do. We were going to be gone for six weeks, and there were things that couldn't wait. (I know what you're thinking. "Why did he let things pile up? Did he procrastinate?")

You could draw your own conclusions if you had seen the state of my desk.

So I went to my office, sat at my desk, and started to work at 9:00 P.M. that night. One hour passed, then two, then three, and the pile of correspondence and bills began to go down. By three o'clock in the morning I felt so good I could have stayed up all night. By 3:30 everything was done. I bounded upstairs, jumped into bed and dozed for an hour. All the following day and far into the next night I was still going strong, having a ball.

Why did I have all that energy when some hours before I had said, "I'm really tired"? Because I saw a job to be done and did it. You have had similar experiences, I'm sure, and know the energy release that is given to you.

Goethe has this to say about that energy release, "Lose this day loitering, 'twill be the same story tomorrow and the next more dilatory. Indecision brings its own delays and days are most lamenting over yesterday. Action—there is courage, magic in it. Anything you can do, or think you can, begin it. Once started, the mind grows heated. Begin the job and the work will be completed."

Time Bank

What if you had a bank that kept a special account for you? Each morning the manager would call and say, "Good morning, we just credited your account with $1,440. Don't forget the conditions. The contract says, 'Whatever part of the money you fail to use during the day will be erased from your account . . . no balance will be brought forward.' Have a happy day using your money."

What would you do? You would be very creative in spending that money. You would draw out every cent every day and use it to the best advantage.

We do have such a bank, and its name is *time*. Every morning it credits you with 1,440 minutes. It says that whatever portion of this you have failed to invest will be lost forever. There is no accumulation of those minutes to be added to tomorrow.

Tomorrow cannot be found on God's calendar.

Tomorrow sounds so innocent, but it is life's most dangerous word.

Tomorrow is the road that leads to the town called NEVER.

The Terrible Twins

Procrastination and frustration are wicked partners. Many of the people who are unhappy and failing to achieve what they want believe they will be successful and happy tomorrow. But tomorrow will be the same as today, because they fail to do anything about their lives now.

There are very few overnight successes. A business flourishes and catches the attention of the public, but what is not seen is that the founders of that business spent years in working and training and trying different ideas. A musician thrills his audience and is proclaimed as a new star. However, he placed an importance on "now" when it came to practicing the boring scales.

Life's Inspiring Four Letter Word

Inherent within the concept of action is the idea of work. Now I realize that *work* is a four letter word that frightens many people. And I don't want to frighten you, but, dynamic living requires work. The right attitude about that will bring inspiration, discipline, energy release and a great deal of sound therapy to the human experience. Henry Ford said, "Work does more than get us our living, it gets us our life." George Bernard Shaw echoed a similar philosophy, "I want to be thoroughly used up, when I die, for the harder I work, the more I live. Life is no brief candle for me. It is a sort of splendid torch which I have got hold of for the moment, and I want to make it burn as brightly as possible before handing it on to future generations." The great composers do not start to work because they are inspired, but become inspired because they are working. They don't waste time waiting for an inspiration.

There is no great excitement and pleasure in having nothing to do; the joy of life is in having lots to do and doing it. In fact, one of the great secrets to having unbounded energy in life is found right here. Get involved in what you're doing, become engrossed in it, dig in, have a variety of things in which to be involved and do it.

Thomas Edison once said, "I'm glad the eight-hour day had not been invented when I was a young man. If my life had been made up of eight-hour days I do not believe I could have accomplished a great deal. This country would not amount to as much as it does if the young men of fifty years ago had been afraid they were doing more than they were being paid for."

The bee making honey visits 125 clover heads to make one gram of sugar: 3,400,000 trips to make one pound of honey!

Leonardo D'Vinci said, "Thou, O God, doth sell to us all good things at the price of labor. Work is the seed from which grows all good things you hope for . . . a man who's afraid of hard work better be brave enough to accept poverty."

Most people in the sales field fail because of the people they fail to see, rather than those they fail to sell.

The foundation for psychological well-being in life is found in this same area. George Shinn says, "Action is indeed therapy. It erases doubts and fears, anxieties and worries. It capitalizes on failures and mistakes and turns them into positive influences. It exercises the mind for problem solving and for creativity. It develops poise under pressure and uses wisdom and experience to consider alternatives and to provide a back-up plan. It calls forth the best in us all, and it becomes the password to success. Action is work, and work is happiness" (*Miracle of Motivation*, p. 238).

An unknown poet put it this way:

If you are rich, work.
If you are burdened with seemingly unfair responsibilities, work.
If you are happy, continue to work.
Idleness gives room for doubts and fears.
If sorrow overwhelms you and loved ones seem not true, work.
If disappointments come, work.
If faith falters and reason fails, just work.
When dreams are shattered and hope seems dead,
Work, work as if your life were in peril;
It really is.

No matter what ails you, work.
Work faithfully and work with faith.
Work is the greatest material remedy available.
Work will cure both mental and physical afflictions.
Work.

Wow! What a boundless promise for a right attitude. I'm not saying one needs to be a "workaholic" or take "guilt trips" at times of leisure. Balance is the key. But right now we're talking about *action*.

What Should I Be Doing Now?

What is the best use of your time right now? What are things you should be doing, but aren't? When tomorrow comes we will pay dearly for what we did not do today, or we will reap bountifully for what we did.

The letter left unanswered.
The bill ignored and unpaid.
The friend you didn't thank.
The lesson never started.
The practice which was forgotten.
The phone call never made.

Each of us will discover an exciting surge of energy by doing those things we have been putting off.

A friend of mine has a card in his office which simply says:
GET GOING . . .
    MOVE . . .
       START . . .
          BEGIN . . .
            ACT . . .
              NOW!

The Bible Says

There is nothing clearer than the Word of God on basic principles. In the book of James it says:

"Look here, you people who say, 'Today or tomorrow we are going to such and such a town, stay there a year, and open up a profitable business.' How do you know what is going to happen tomorrow? For the length of your lives is as uncertain as the morning fog—now you see it; soon it is gone" (James 4:13, 14, TLB).

Now is the time! Do it now!

10

BELIEVE IT BEFORE YOU SEE IT

Principle #7: Principle of Faith
"Faith is the substance of things hoped for, the evidence of things not seen" (Hebrews 11:1).

When I began teaching the Dynamic Living Seminars I did not speak specifically on the principle of faith. That does not mean I had nothing to do with it, nor that I did not believe in it. In fact, it stood as the foundation stone of my whole approach to life. The principle was so essential and obvious to me that for many years I assumed everyone knew, understood, and applied this powerful truth.

Then I discovered there are many people who simply memorize a list of principles and hope for the best. By sheer strength of rote memory, dumb luck, or even disciplined study, they wish for their dreams to come true. I know, as so many do, that faith is an absolute necessity. Faith is the essential ingredient in all of the principles we have listed. If you don't believe they will work, there is no point in trying to apply them to your life. The principles are not on trial, but lack of faith in them will destroy their effectiveness.

In taking a look at the definition of faith in the dictionary we find the primary meaning to be: "Believing without proof; trust." The illuminating description which follows that definition is the same statement we used at the beginning of this chapter from Hebrews. It is difficult to depart from biblical illustrations when we begin to talk about faith.

When Susan and I were in the Holy Land, we stood at the ruins of a city called Jericho. Even my friends who don't know much about the Old Testament can sing a line from that great spiritual which says, "Joshua fit the battle of Jericho." (Some people might prefer to say "fought," but I've always sung it the way it's written and find it awkward to change.) Remember the wall that came tumbling down? Joshua didn't have dynamite, or some heavy, ancient ramming rod. He had something even stronger: Joshua had faith.

Joshua had been leading the children of Israel into the Promised Land when the Lord told him to take the city of Jericho. He didn't tell Joshua to try to take the city. He told him explicitly, "I have given Jericho into your hand."

However, God gave Joshua some unusual instructions. Can you imagine the challenges Joshua had when he told his people what they were going to do? With a perfectly straight face, because Joshua didn't see anything strange in God's instructions, he told the Israelites that they would leave the camp each day and march around Jericho without saying a word.

I've often wondered why he gave those instructions. Sometimes I think it was because he was afraid someone would come out with doubting statements which would throw a negative pall over the whole crowd. They might begin to mumble, "What kind of a crazy leader is this Joshua? How does he expect us to win a battle by marching around a wall? They're probably armed to the teeth inside there, just waiting for us to go inside and be zapped."

To make matters more exciting, they were told to march around seven times. On the seventh day, Joshua said, "Okay, ready now . . . shout and blow the trumpets, the battle is won and the city is ours."

Before a word was said or one blast had been sounded from the horns, Joshua made a statement of faith. He had God's promise before he experienced the results. The people shouted, the priests blew the trumpets, and the walls fell as flat as a cold soufflé. Israelites leaped over the rubble and went straight ahead to take the city.

When was the battle won? Not when the trumpets sounded; not when the people shouted; not when the march started or even when they invaded the city. The victory came in advance when Joshua told them, "The city is ours."

Faith shouts the victory before the battle ever begins!

"The power of believing. The power of faith. It is the most impressive part of man, the most highly developed, the source of our greatest energy. God gave us superb physical equipment. He gave us brains like computers, eyes that can see many miles, muscles that can lift heavy weights, skin that repairs itself, a heart that pumps blood thousands of times an hour, day after day, for dozens of years, seldom missing a beat.

"God gave us lots of impressive equipment, but skin and bones and tissue and glands and muscles are not what man is all about. Lower animals have all those things. What makes man unique is the ability to believe, to have faith, to see the unseen; and that power to believe is man's most powerful property. It is the best and brightest part of man.

"So when you hear about the power of believing, or the 'magic' of believing, or the 'miracle' of believing, or such phrases as that, don't dismiss it too quickly as just so much talk, just so much rhetoric from the positive-thinking preachers. The power to believe is much more than a catchphrase, more than just words from one of those success-and-motivation books. It is as real as—and much more important than—hair and skin and arms and legs and the other parts of man that are visible" (*Making It Happen*, p. 59).

Faith is the pillar of strength that allows men to achieve the impossible, reach the unattainable, and solve the unfathomable.

Faith in What?

We are living in the day of the scientific approach. We are taught that if we can't see it, taste it, touch it, hear it, smell it, or in some objective manner substantiate it, then we should reject it as not true. Faith does not counteract the scientific approach, it just takes a step beyond. In fact, William Adams said, "Faith is the continuation of reason." Faith says: I believe it, whether I have any evidence or not! Ralph Waldo Emerson said: "All I have seen teaches me to trust the Creator for all I have not seen."

Every day we place our faith in objects that have earned the right to our faith because of past performance. We sit on a chair with faith that it won't break. We turn on the tap with faith that water will stream out. And yet we may pollute our conversation with such phrases as, "It's just impossible to believe in anyone or anything today."

Where do we place our faith, if it is so essential to success in life? I believe that the foundation of faith is in God and the words of faith are in the Bible. Study all the great books of the ages, consider all the wise leaders, and none will compare to the ageless best seller, the Bible.

Where Do I Begin?

In the little Danish town of Solvang, California, there's a restaurant whose name caught my eye. It's called The Mustard Seed. Some people wonder where the owners got such an unusual name, until they find out it came from another great faith passage which says, "If you have faith as a mustard seed, you shall say to this mountain, 'Move from here to there,' and it shall move; and nothing shall be impossible to you" (Matthew 17:20, NASB).

People have said, "I wish I had your faith." My faith is very small, but my God is powerful. Men and women of great faith are those who know that possibility thinking is belief in the God of the impossible. Faith is believing in what God says, simply because it is God who says it. Faith works in our lives as God works in our faith.

Meanwhile Back at the Ranch

Circle A Ranch is a working example of faith in the God who works the impossible feats. Susan and I had one obstacle after another thrown in the path of obtaining the ranch and opening it. When we saw the ranch house, the swimming pool, the barn and corrals, when we looked over the beautiful rolling hills of Michigan, we knew this was the place of our dreams. With no previous experience in running a camp, we launched into the project and learned as we went. The greatest challenge came, however, when we had arranged the financing, had the first batch of kids coming, and then apparently were blocked by the townspeople. It was a heated crowd of concerned citizens who gathered to question what sort of an organization we had. Rumors had been flying through the little town that we were some sort of a cult, and the good citizens did not want their peaceful village contaminated. (I agreed with them!)

Fortunately, some of our business associates lived in this same area. They began to talk with many of our potential neighbors, shared our albums and tapes with them and turned the tide. We opened on time! All the steps we took, all the decisions we made seemed to be such small moves at the time. But they led to a great outreach.

We knew we had been led into this project and had faith that God would work it out.

Faith Is Being Receptive

Someone said, "God without man is still God. Man without God is nothing."

Mark Twain once said that one of the greatest women who ever lived was Helen Keller. Recently I came across a little book called *The Faith of Helen Keller,* in which this remarkable person tells about her beliefs. Helen Keller was imprisoned in a world where she could neither hear nor see. And yet, she lectured throughout the world, wrote many books, learned several languages, and became a friend of the world's most famous people.

She wrote: "A simple, childlike faith in a Divine Friend solves all the problems that come to us by land or sea" (p. 28).

"Faith does not oblige us to be unusually endowed, but receptive. To say others may have it but we cannot is wanton self-limitation. To be alert for whatever surprises may glow within us is to have at our command a zest for living which outweighs all material possessions'' (p. 28).

Try closing your eyes and blocking your ears to sound. This was Helen Keller's world, and yet she escaped her prison with belief in God, belief in herself, and belief in others. She learned to hope, to trust, to love, and to be happy through faith.

The blind with their hand in God's can see more clearly than those of us who can see but have no faith.

When my girls were small I would say to them, as all fathers do, "Come on, honey, jump. Daddy will catch you." They may have been afraid, but they knew they could trust me. They had absolute faith that I wouldn't let them crash to the floor. That is the simple, childlike faith that the Father requires of us. He will carry us and not let us down. But first, we need to take that leap of faith.

Not "If," but "When"

Many people go through life pushing the "if" button. "If everything falls together I'll get the contract." "If the weather is nice, I'll call on my customers." "If I could just see it, I'd believe it."

There's a great "if" story in the Bible about a distressed father who brought his demon-possessed son to Jesus and said, "If you can do anything, take pity on us and help us."

There was an "if" in the question, but the poor father had put it in the wrong place. Without demanding that the man retract the "if" Jesus kindly put it in its proper position. He said, "What do you mean, 'If you can?' Everything is possible for him who believes" (Mark 9:23, NIV).

Jesus seemed to be saying that there should be no "if" about his power, or his willingness to help. If we believe, all things are possible!

> Doubt sees the obstacles;
> Faith sees the way.
> Doubt sees the darkest night;

Faith sees the day.
Doubt dreads to take a step;
Faith soars on high.
Doubt questions, "Who believes?"
Faith answers, "I."
                          Author Unknown

Believe in Yourself

The truly self-assured person is God-assured. As we set our faith priorities, belief in yourself is next in line; it is faith in your ability, your worth, and your talents, knowing that God has given you gifts you haven't used yet!

If we don't have faith for the large tasks of life, we can develop faith in ourselves for each small job that leads us to our determined destination.

In chapter 14 we'll discuss this belief in more detail.

Believe in Others

A wise man said, "The man who trusts men will make fewer mistakes than he who distrusts them."

One of my friends said he uses the "vowel principle" in dealing with people. He says, "I O U *a*cceptance and *e*ncouragement." When you have faith in God, and faith in yourself, it is easier to have faith in others.

What do we crave in order to live? Psychologists have studied thousands of cases of people with all kinds of problems, and concluded that people are starved for recognition. Ego-hunger is as natural as hunger for food. What happens to the man who normally eats three meals a day, is good-natured and jolly, when he is denied food for a time? He snaps at his wife and the kids, and is downright grumpy. His mind is on his stomach, and it doesn't do any good to tell him to think about something else. The only cure is to feed him.

The same is true of feeding someone's ego-hunger. If a person is starved for self-esteem, he can't get his mind off himself and give his attention to others.

When we believe in others, we make them feel important. Men and women who believe other people are important have gained one of the keys to a successful life. Why are people important, anyhow? Because every single person was created in the image of God! That makes him important.

When we believe in others, we notice them. One of the reasons children misbehave is that they want to be noticed. Every mother knows that a child seems to choose the time when she is on the telephone to crawl on the countertop and drop the jar of jelly. We all crave attention, whether we admit it or not.

In our business people are recognized with pins for levels of achievement, with trips and awards for their accomplishments. Many people who go to an Amway meeting for the first time are amazed by the number of standing ovations people receive. Recognition comes from the top and filters into every level of the organization. People thrive on being noticed!

Acceptance is an important ingredient in believing in others. People who accept people just as they are, without trying to change them, usually have more influence over changing that person's behavior for the better than the person who is supercritical and demanding. My wife Susan has heard me speak hundreds of times. She sits through hours and hours of repeated seminars, listening to the same talks over and over again. She is such an encouragement, because her rapt attention just says to me, "Whatever you say, honey, I believe you."

If people were accepted by their mates, their parents, their business associates, they would find it easier to accept themselves and be on the way to self-improvement.

My father-in-law, who became very successful in the business world, knew the power of faith in these areas of life. So often did he speak of the necessity to believe, that in spite of the fact he has been gone for more than a decade, displayed in a prominent place in the homes of some of his associates, you can still find his picture with the caption, "You must believe."

Faith Is Total Commitment

A life of faith takes total commitment. Faith in God, yourself, and others is a way of walking, not just talking.

A man decided he was going to walk across Niagara Falls on a tightrope. He started to practice and rigged up a little working area in his back yard. First he placed the rope about eighteen inches off the ground and began to balance back and forth. Gradually, he raised the rope higher and higher until he was thirty-five feet in the air. Then he added chairs, wheelbarrows and bicycles to his act. Soon word of his ambitious goal reached the newspapers, and they sent out a reporter to watch him work. His fame grew and people began to make bets on his ability to accomplish this feat.

One day his neighbor came over and said, "You know, I believe you're ready to do it."

The tightrope walker said, "What makes you think so?"

"I've been watching you almost every day since you started. You're very good. In fact, you are extremely talented. I think you can walk across Niagara Falls on a rope. I have faith in you."

He was encouraged. "Do you really?" he asked with a big smile.

"I certainly do. You're ready."

"That's marvelous. I decided the same thing today. In fact, I'm making preparations right now to get the line set up across the Falls and tomorrow is the big day. As long as you have faith in my ability to do it, why don't we do this? I'll take a wheelbarrow up and you get in it and I'll wheel you across."

Now *that* would be total commitment! That is what the principle of faith is all about. It appears that we are right back to the principle of the preceding chapter—action. Faith is not a complete concept unless accompanied by action. Faith makes a difference. When we believe, we are willing to do things to make that commitment. The apostle James said it: "Faith without deeds is dead" (James 2:26, NIV).

Here are some seed thoughts on faith:

"Faith is to believe what we do not see, and the reward of this faith is to see what we believe" *St. Augustine.*

Our grand business in life is not to see what lies dimly at a distance, but to do what lies clearly at hand. God will supply, but we must apply.

Just before we move on let me challenge you in the faith experience of life. Is that a dimension in which you move? Where is your faith placed? Are you moving mountains or getting buried? Only he who can see the invisible can do the impossible.

11

SOME VERVE!

Principle #8: The Principle of Enthusiasm
"Put everything you've got into everything you do."

A few years ago my speech-making was about as exciting as reading the telephone directory. My words were clear and my enunciation precise. Sentences were put together in logical sequence, and thoughts were conveyed clearly. But the enthusiastic communication process that characterizes my talks today had not yet begun. In fact, my business was reflecting the same lack of enthusiasm.

Enthusiasm can be taught, and when it is, it will be caught. When I give a speech today, I laugh (some people call it a giggle and that's okay with me), shout, pace the platform, and pour all the bodily energy I can into a talk. I am frequently asked how I can maintain that energy for such long periods of time. One reason is that I am extremely enthusiastic about the dynamic living principles. If I'm not enthusiastic, no one else will be.

Results in any endeavor in life come in direct proportion to enthusiasm. Robert Schuller put it this way, "Enthusiasm is the propellant power that will take you from a slow liftoff into a steady, upward surge. With its controlled, explosive jet force you'll put your dreams in orbit! It turns 'have-nots' into 'have-its.' It turns starters into finishers. It takes underdogs and makes them champions.''

Emerson said that nothing great was ever achieved without enthusiasm.

Enthusiasm is one of the key attitudes for success.

Teach It to the Young

Small children are enthusiastic little beings. Unfortunately they begin to encounter the enthusiasm squelchers. They hear, "Calm down, now." "Don't get so excited." "Take it easy." By the time they reach junior high many of them have reached the "cool" stage. It's more acceptable to complain and yawn, rather than do a job eagerly.

Isn't it tragic? We have developed the attitude that there are only a few times, places, or events where it is appropriate to be enthusiastic. We're talking about the freedom to give all you've got, enthusiastically, to every experience of your life!

Enthusiasm comes from the Greek *en theos* and literally means "God in us." That can generate a lot of excitement in me. How about you? We usually think of enthusiasm in other terms. There are athletic contests, for instance, where there's a lot of loud, noisy cheering or the applause for an outstanding performance. There's nothing wrong with cheering, but that's not what we are primarily concerned with now. Enthusiasm is an attitude, a way of life.

When the kids come to Circle A Ranch many of them think it will be two weeks of riding horses, swimming, and doing all those fun things you do at camp. "You mean I have to work?" is the startled question, either voiced or unspoken. Suddenly they discover it is a working ranch.

There are weeds to be pulled, the fence to be painted, stalls to be cleaned. Some of these kids had never done anything harder than emptying the wastebasket at home, and then we tell them to rake the gravel paths and scrub the floors.

It's wonderful to watch the development of attitude as we begin to teach these concepts. When we get to the principle of enthusiasm, we say, "Put everything you've got into everything you do." During the last few days of the session when we announce the work projects, the whole group shouts, "Yeah!" It's fun to see fifty kids get excited about sweeping floors, washing windows and shoveling manure. Their enthusiasm is so contagious that when their parents come for the final banquet and the boys and girls take them around to show the work they've done, many of those moms and dads can't believe it.

Your Enthusiasm Is Showing

You've probably heard, "To be enthusiastic, act enthusiastic." Perhaps you don't feel like being enthusiastic. You've just had some bad news, you are depressed over something that has happened, and the thought of being enthusiastic is repulsive to you. You don't have to jump up and down or wave a flag to be enthusiastic. It is an inward attitude which shows in your face, your voice, and the movements of your body. We all owe it to each other to be enthusiastic.

A friend of mine from Canada, Jim Janz, tells about the time he returned from the funeral of a family member and was reminded that he had to fly to Seattle for a speech he had promised to make before a large crowd. He was depressed and wanted to cancel that engagement, but knew they were expecting him. On the plane, instead of dwelling upon his own sadness, he began to affirm, "I am really excited about speaking for these people. I am enthusiastic about the audience." He used the principle of command to spark his attitude and when he rose to speak at the rally his first words were, "Boy, am I excited to be here."

Have you ever wondered why some churches are packed and others are dwindling? Of course, the basic teaching from the pulpits should be sound, but without enthusiastic belief in the subject matter, and clear presentation of the message, the pastor will lose his following. Enthusiasm is one of the keys for success in our growing, vibrant churches today.

Step One to Enthusiasm: Do Your Homework

Someone said, "We're down on what we're not up on."

One of the keys to enthusiasm is to learn about the thing you aren't enthusiastic about. It doesn't matter what the subject might be, there is no way you can convey excitement or enthusiasm about it if you haven't done your homework.

Bob and Sally like to travel. When you are around them, the sense of adventure, the smells and sights of different lands and cultures, comes alive. Before you know it, you're ready to dig into savings, call the travel agent, and hop the next plane. Why? Because they devour travel folders and books about a particular country before they begin their journey. They know what to look for in the art of that region, what the choice of ethnic food is, and where to search for the bargains. They do their homework so well before a trip that they are able to savor the journey.

On the other hand, I have met people in my travels who complain about everything. The wonderful experiences of going to new places and meeting different people are lost in the emphasis upon the little things that go wrong. When they tell you about their trip you resolve never to go to that place.

Enthusiasm is developed by finding out about the person, the subject, or the place. David Schwartz in his book, *The Magic of Thinking Big,* calls it the "dig-into-it-deeper technique."

We can test ourselves with this question, "What are one or two things in which I have no enthusiasm?" Think about it. Are you interested in classical ballet or Arabian horses or baseball? Chances are if you are negative about any of those subjects you know very little about them.

Have you ever heard a boy in love describe his girl friend to someone? She's an incredible creature. She designs and makes her own clothes; she jogs on the beach every day; she has the most sympathetic listening ear. The young man in love can spend hours learning everything about this remarkable person. His enthusiasm is boundless.

When Susan and I were married, I knew very little about horses. She had been riding since she was a child, but I didn't know a bridle from a stirrup. However, we were given sixteen Arabian horses for our ranch, and I needed to find out about raising horses.

I had been on a horse twice before in my life—once when I was thirteen, and that lasted about thirteen seconds when the horse and I parted company. It took more than the next thirteen years to get me on another horse. In fact, our older daughter Cindy was past thirteen. We were on a family trip in Glacier National Park and the family convinced me I could do it. A one hour trail ride on a horse who knew he was supposed to keep his nose on the tail of the horse in front of him proved that I could ride.

Then came Circle A Ranch and all those horses! I had no choice. However, as I have worked with the horses and learned what beautiful animals they are, all my former fears have vanished. I can help with any of the procedures necessary in their care, feeding, and breeding, and I'll ride any horse we have. I've done my horse homework!

We have some beautiful horses at the ranch and some day we'll have them in national competition.

To be enthusiastic, fall in love with your subject.

Step Two to Enthusiasm: Do It with Verve

Enthusiasm shows in everything we do. For instance, watch the way people walk. The person who relishes life, who meets each day with energy and a sense of expectancy, walks faster and stands taller. Why do entertainers run on stage? Why do speakers step quickly to the podium? They are giving themselves enthusiastically to their audiences.

If you walk with eyes downcast, shoulders slumped, you are communicating discouragement. Your body can convey despair or joy.

The way a person walks and stands shows confidence or insecurity. A confident attitude will attract others and inspire them. Walk as if you have someplace to go and you know where you're going. Follow the advice we have given our children, "Stand up straight, don't slump." We are judged by the body language we portray. Walk and move with verve!

My mother-in-law is Bernice Hansen, one of America's outstanding businesswomen. She is past what used to be considered retirement age, but when she walks in a room she radiates such enthusiasm that people are attracted to her immediately. You will never see her slump, no matter how tired she might be.

Next, put verve in your handshake. The person with the cold fish handshake probably has a low self-esteem. The one who grips your hand in a vise and drives your ring into your flesh may be compensating for a lack of self-confidence. A handshake should be a little squeeze, but not a bone-crusher. Some people greet by grasping your hand with both of their hands. It conveys a warm message that says, "I like you, you're special."

Put verve in your smile. Recently I attended a church where the choir director was directing the singing about the joy of the Lord. He never smiled once. A smile was designed by God for human beings to give away, not hoard. A smile may lift another heart out of despondency. A smile doesn't cost you anything, and yet it may lead to success and riches. A smile says, "You're important. I like you."

Why do we love our dog and smile at him? Because when he sees us he nearly jumps out of his skin, wagging his tail to tell us that he's glad to see us.

An insincere grin is worse than no smile at all. A real, heart-warming smile that comes from within and shines through the eyes will bring a very high price in the marketplace of life.

Some seed thoughts:

What sunshine is to flowers, smiles are to humanity.

Be cheerful. Of all the things you wear, your expression is the most important.

One of the best things a man can have up his sleeve is a funny bone.

> How many smiles from day to day
> I've missed along my narrow way!
> How many kindly words I've lost
> What joy has my indifference cost!
> This glorious friend that now I know
> Would have been friendly years ago.
> *Author Unknown*

Someone asked me, "But, Skip, what if I don't feel like smiling?'' I asked him a question, ''Do you think Sammy Davis, Jr. always feels like smiling?'' It's not what you feel like doing, it's what you should be doing. Force yourself to smile. Soon you'll be smiling, because the law of giving has gone into effect. When you give the smile, someone will smile back at you. It's almost impossible to be worried and anxious when you're smiling.

One of the best pieces of advice I ever received was when I was told to smile mentally before my lips moved. Feel ''smiley'' inside. Let yourself go. If you have trouble feeling that smile from inside, go through the motions, anyhow. Look in the mirror and smile at yourself. If your teeth aren't straight, don't worry about it. Practice in front of the mirror until you see a genuine smile returning to you.

I know a woman who was meeting the husband of a good friend at the airport. The man, Ron, had never seen his wife's friend before, but he walked right up to her in the crowd. ''How on earth did you know me?'' she asked.

''Easy. My wife just told me to look for the gal with the big smile, and there you were.''

> A smile is cheer to you and me
> The cost is nothing—it's given free
> It comforts the weary—gladdens the sad
> Consoles those in trouble—good or bad.
> To rich and poor—beggar or thief
> It's free to all of any belief.
> A natural gesture of young and old
> Cheers on the faint—disarms the bold.
> Unlike most blessing for which we pray
> It's one thing we keep when we give it away.
> *Author Unknown*

Put verve in your speech. When I first started the Dynamic Living Seminars, I hid behind a podium and spoke carefully into the microphone. My church background showed as I spoke from the comfort of a pulpit. I could hold on with both hands and not have to worry about what to do with my arms. My knees could be comfortably locked and no one would know the difference.

Then I was introduced to a wiry guy who was a choreographer for some of the top dancing stars in the business. He had danced with fellows like Gene Kelly, so you know he was good. He was one of the most enthusiastic people I have ever met. He had to be, because he taught this stiff, awkward preacher's kid to dance. In the process, Alex also taught me how to move. I don't mean just to get from one place to another, I mean really moooooove! When I began to pick up the mike and walk around the platform when I spoke, my voice became more enthusiastic.

It doesn't matter who you are talking to: the PTA, a business group, your children, or your spouse, putting vitality into your voice will inspire others.

A secretary who answers the phone with enthusiasm is worth more to her boss than one who is a great typist. A salesman will get more appointments when his voice conveys enthusiasm than the one with a monotone on a low key.

Have you ever called someone on the phone and had them answer with, "Hullo"? It's so far down in the basement that you can feel the dampness. Practice putting verve into your voice. Record yourself and listen to your voice. If you were sitting in an audience where you were speaking would you be uplifted or deflated?

Stop for a moment or two right now and consider what would happen if you went to work tomorrow morning and with great enthusiasm declared for all to hear, "I am so excited to be here today . . . I could hardly wait to arrive. I am so charged with enthusiasm for my job I'm excited to begin! This is going to be a *great day!*"

Would that affect your attitude, your job, your boss, your fellow workers? What if everyone came in with that enthusiastic approach? Would production increase? You bet it would.

Are you an employer? How would your people feel if, with enthusiasm, you told them each morning how great they are and how grateful you are that they are with you? Hey, a lot of difficulties in our economy today would be a thing of the past if we could get this type of enthusiasm saturating our businesses.

Charlie "Tremendous" Jones says, "A lot of people think

enthusiasm or a cheerful spirit is something that falls on you. I want to tell you this with all my heart; the most challenging thing you'll ever face in your life is learning every day to be excited about what you're doing." (*Life Is Tremendous*, p. 25).

Be a Good News Broadcaster

Years ago the newscaster, Lowell Thomas, made himself famous by beginning his radio programs with, "There's good news tonight." He got our attention, because we like good news.

When the kids burst in from school and say, "The greatest thing happened at school today," we are at attention. Good news develops enthusiasm; it helps our physical well-being. A friend told me about his son who always began his prayers with, "Thank you, Lord, for this beautiful day." It could be dark and hailing outside, but he looked at every day as being great.

A good news broadcaster is the person who says, "I feel great," when you ask him how he is. He can tell funny stories on himself and laugh at himself. Although he never laughs at the problems of others.

A good friend of mine decided that the response he needs to make to the question, "How are you?," must be filled with enthusiasm. He replies with great strength and conviction, many times with a loud voice and clap of hands, "Greatest day of my life, friend, how about you?"

Needless to say, he gets some amazed reactions. One day in a bank he faced another customer with that response and question. The other man stammered and stuttered, finally getting out, "I guess so."

"Well, it better be!" my friend replied.

"Why?" the bewildered customer said.

"Because yesterday is gone, tomorrow hasn't come, and today's the only day you've got. It has to be the greatest day of your life!"

One sage said, "Don't spend your days stringing and tuning your instrument—start making music now."

To be the person people want to be around, we need to be alive, enthusiastic people.

Ooze enthusiasm. We call it enthuzeoozeoozeoozeasm!

The Bible says, "When a man is gloomy, everything seems to go wrong; when he is cheerful, everything seems right!" (Proverbs 15:13, TLB).

12

DO IT ANYHOW

Principle #9: Principle of Self-discipline
"Do what needs to be done when it ought to be done, whether you like it or not."

Why are good words and right concepts turned into villains? Take discipline, for instance. Because there are harsh behavior patterns, such as child abuse and wife-beating, many people look upon discipline as a dirty word. Oppressive and unloving punishment are wrong, but they do not give us reasons to justify lack of discipline. In fact, real love includes the willingness to instruct, guide, teach, and discipline.

Before we began to write this book, my co-author, Carole Carlson, visited our Circle A ranch and interviewed many of the kids. She commented, "I was amazed that these boys and girls responded so positively to the exact guidelines established at the camp. One boy said that Skip's program was more precisely structured than any camp he had ever attended, but he added, 'Golly, the work projects make me feel worthwhile.'"

At Circle A we instill the advantages of discipline in the kids.

They thrive on it. "There is a mistaken notion prevailing among some parents that discipline is the same thing as punishment. It is not. Discipline comes from a Latin word meaning 'to teach.' The best discipline is that which teaches" (*How Christian Parents Face Family Problems*, p. 37).

I believe the parents of this generation of young people have experienced some of the disastrous results of their own permissive upbringing and the pendulum is beginning to swing back to raising children in a tradition of respect for elders, respect for rules, and respect for themselves. There are hundreds of thousands of young people across our nation today, looking for someone who loves them enough to say, "This is the way, walk in it." It's not an attitude that approaches with the clenched fist of demand, but with the open hand of love which reaches out to say, "Come on, follow me. I'll show you the way."

Dr. James Dobson, the prominent child psychologist, wrote: "It should come as no surprise that our beloved children have hangups; we have sacrificed this generation on the altar of overindulgence, permissiveness, and smother-love. Certainly, other factors have contributed to the present unsettled youth scene, but I believe the major cause has been related to the anarchy that existed in millions of American homes" (*Dare to Discipline*, p. 22).

Where Does Discipline Begin?

It's a common scene in the supermarket. Darling little Snuggums wants some candy, and Mother says, "No." Snuggums then stands up in the cart, jeopardizing both herself and the groceries, and begins to wail. All eyes turn on Snuggums, and her mother, embarrassed and anxious to quiet her screaming child, says, "Here, Snuggums, take a piece . . . and stop your crying." Snuggums has won a small battle, and in her little mind she knows that the way to get what she wants is to make a scene.

One of the greatest gifts we can give to our children is consistent and certain discipline. Idle threats, such as, "If you do that one more time I'll whip you," create severe difficulties for both parent and child when they are not carried through. The child is smart enough to figure out when "one more" means "one more time."

Discipline is directed toward bad behavior. It should never be delivered in the heat of emotion, but should be followed by loving reassurance. It's not my purpose to elaborate on discipline in the home. However, where does self-discipline begin? When we are small, we have no self-discipline; it has to be learned. This is an on-going process which teaches us the wisdom of establishing limits to our behavior. Ideally, that begins in the home.

As we grow older, we go to school and have to attend classes for a certain number of hours. The discipline is imposed by teachers and school rules. Then Johnny gets out of school and is in the big, competitive world of business. He is disciplined by his job to be at work at eight, take a one hour lunch break, and stay until five. Most of his self-discipline is regulated by others.

However, when Johnny is out of the office, no one is telling him what to do. His challenge is to discipline himself. Where and how does Johnny spend his time? Where does he apply his mind and his talents? What will motivate him, or any other person, to do what needs to be done?

A person's difficulties begin when he or she is able to do as he likes.

We can't separate discipline and desire. If the desire is strong enough, if it is burning within you to achieve a goal, the discipline can be developed.

I am so impressed by the self-discipline of athletes. A few years ago, when Mark Spitz won seven gold medals and set seven world records in swimming, I thought, *Boy, wouldn't it be marvelous to be a natural swimmer like that?* What about the young people who break records in the Olympic competitions? What we don't see is that every morning in swim clubs across the nation, those little kids, seven, eight, nine years old, hit the water at six o'clock and swim back and forth for two or three hours. Then they get out of the water, go off to school all day, and come back to hit the water for another three hours before dinner. Seven days a week they practice. Why? Driving their bodies to the point of extreme strain,

they develop their abilities to the fullest extent. When the moment
of competition comes, their self-discipline pays off.

During the Olympic competition, the Japanese gymnastic team
knew they had a good chance of winning the gold medal. As they
went into the competition, their expectations were high, as the
team scored well. The time came for the competition of the rings,
which involves some fancy manuevers on those rings which hang
from ceiling-high ropes. A young man who is world class in his
ability in that particular event, came out and grabbed the rings; he
pulled himself up and started his routine. He twisted, turned,
manuevered through the dislocates into the power move of the iron
cross, holding himself steady while the crowd and the judges
scrutinized his every move. Then came the final moment of his
routine, and the twisting, turning dismount sent him into the air.
Until that point, every motion had been perfect. Then it happened—that dreaded moment that must loom like an awesome
spector to every competitor. He came down, and as he landed, his
arms shot into the air, pain racked his body, and he crumpled into a
heap.

He was rushed to a hospital and X-rays revealed his right knee
was shattered. The next day his team mates came in, full of excitement, and said, "We've got a chance at the gold medal! We can
win it! If you'll just come back and do one more performance,
we'll win!"

That athlete must have looked at his knee, swathed in bandages
and throbbing from the injury, and thought, *I can't do it, it's
impossible.* Instead he said, "I'll try."

They loaded him into the ambulance, informing him of the
encouraging news. "For us to win, you're going to have to score a
9.5!" Since that was better than he had ever done in world competition, the possibility must have looked slim. They helped him
into the center ring, and steadied him as he reached for the rings.
All the hours of discipline that had forced his body to the point of
absolute agony and exhaustion began to take over. He grabbed the
rings and pulled himself up. Twisting, turning, into the power
move, the iron cross, a few more dislocates, another power move,
and then came the final moment. He went up, turned, and came

down with full force on both feet, onto the floor; his arms shot into the air, pain wracked his body, but he held the position. The judges' cards went up slowly. The crowd was hushed in silence as the points were read: 9.4, 9.5, 9.5, 9.5, 9.5, 9.6. The Japanese team had won the gold medal!

"Natural" athletes are people of discipline. Arnold Palmer practiced eight hours a day, day after day, using the same club to hit two thousand balls one after the other. And when he walks out on a golf course somebody says, "Wouldn't it be fun to be a natural golfer like that?"

I have a good friend who is a pianist. After a brilliant rendition of "Rhapsody in Blue" before several thousand people, one woman in the audience said, "I'd love to be able to play like Jan." Would that admirer be willing to start playing the piano at age three, practice six or eight hours a day, walk on stage with a raging fever and perform flawlessly?

Begin with Those Things You Can Control

Often people give up on choosing a course of self-discipline by concentrating only on the vastness of the commitment. Sometimes it's helpful to start with those things over which you have control. If the marathon runner considers the total length of his race before he ever starts training, he may never begin. He can, however, decide to start with the first mile and add greater distance each week.

To be a vivacious, enthusiastic extrovert with the charisma that attracts people may seem way out of reach. But we all know that smiling is a part of that. A person could start by determining to smile at three people each day. We can control our smile. To be the top salesman in the country may seem unrealistic, but we can control the discipline to make three calls every day. Start someplace.

Will You Pay the Price?

Whether we're talking about home, business, physical, or mental life, there are things we say we want, but we aren't willing to do what needs to be done to have them. There's a price to be paid for success in any area of life.

For instance, what is your time worth? Have you paid the price to learn how to manage the days, hours, and minutes given to you? It has been said that the average person who has lived to be seventy years of age has spent his time in the following manner: three years in education, eight years in amusement, six years in waiting, eleven years in working, twenty-four years in sleeping, five and a half years in conversation, three years in reading, and only six months in church.

Since you are above average, why not compete with yourself on disciplining your minutes, hours and days? Again, the discipline has no meaning without goals.

When do you want to finish your housework?

When do you want to make enough money for your church, or charity, or something you desire to buy for your family?

When do you want to finish the project you started last year?

Here are some guidelines for time discipline. I'm not saying I have mastered all of them, but knowing what to do is certainly the first step toward doing it.

We cannot do everything at once; but we can do something at once.

1. Get up fifteen minutes earlier and know what you're going to wear that day.
2. Increase your reading and writing skills . . . learn to read faster and write notes more promptly.
3. Develop the habit of making good notes. Keep reference files to guide you in your activities.
4. Be decisive. Act fast.
5. Control your telephone.
6. Don't get bogged down in details. Some say, "Don't major in minors."
7. Get the important and hard jobs done first. (Have a list of "Things to Do Today," prioritize them, and get started.)
8. Look for short cuts.
9. Learn to take a break. One of the worst time stealers is to be harassed and tired.
10. Stop daydreaming and do it.

Do It Anyhow

Self-discipline is doing what needs to be done, when it ought to be done, whether you like it or not.

Many times people think of bad habits they would like to replace with good habits. For instance, smoking is a habit that many find difficult to stop, and yet they would like to give it up. One person said, "To cease smoking is the easiest thing I ever did. I ought to know, I've done it a thousand times." *The Reader's Digest* (November, 1982) had a story called "Death of a Surgeon," which graphically documented the progression of lung cancer in Dr. Paul Adkins, a nationally recognized thoracic surgeon. A man of great discipline in his work and studies, he was a victim of the very disease he had concentrated on in his long career in medicine. Before he died a friend asked if he had any regrets, and the doctor answered, "Just one. I regret not quitting smoking twenty years ago."

What are your challenges of self-discipline? On occasion I've had to say to myself, "Skip, if you don't discipline yourself in this part of your life, you will have to suffer the consequences." (Smoking has never been one of my challenges, but there are others. I choose not to speak them into existence by listing what they are.)

I've had people come up to me and speak about what they didn't like to do in our business. The answer: Do it anyhow. "I don't like to retail the products." Do it anyhow. "I hate to go to meetings." Do it anyhow. "I don't enjoy going to seminars where I'm told to do it anyhow." Good, do it anyhow.

What will motivate you to study and apply the principles outlined in this book? Where has (or will) the self-discipline come from to cause you to do what needs to be done in order to move you in to the exhilarating experience known as dynamic living?

It has often been noted by those involved in human motivation that there are three major forms of motivation: (1) Fear: "Do it or suffer the consequences." (2) Reward. (3) A change of inner attitude: "I'll do it because I choose to do it." The learning process we cited earlier in this chapter, where discipline is applied by outside forces at home, school, and job, is based upon the first two. If you have been (or will be) smart enough to develop priorities and a value structure that incorporate the wisdom of self-discipline, then you can live with the finest of all motivation, the proper inner attitude! You will know, as every self-disciplined person knows, there is always a price to pay for success, but it is never as great as the price you pay for failure!

The Bible says, "No discipline seems pleasant at the time, but painful. Later on, however, it produces a harvest of righteousness and peace for those who have been trained by it" (Hebrews 12:11, NIV).

13

DO IT UNTIL

Principle #10: Principle of Persistence
"I will until."

We have some close friends in California who waited thirteen years before their first baby was born. They were so excited when their little one came along that they turned her into one of the most photographed babies I've ever known. Every Tuesday was designated as photography day. On that day, without fail, their little girl had her picture taken. It was not just one picture but a whole roll! We are given the opportunity of viewing those pictures every time we visit them.

When I think about the time when little Tricia Ann was ready to walk, I know that her parents were ready to record that moment for all of posterity. They had the movie camera ready, the still camera poised, the tape recorder rolling, ready to capture every movement and every sound with the best technological apparatus they could buy. Everything was in readiness for Tricia's debut. Mom was standing on one side of the room, holding onto her baby's hand and softly encouraging her, "Okay, sweetheart, go to Daddy." On the other side of the room, proudly grinning, Daddy called her, "Come on, Tricia, come to Daddy. Come on, baby."

All Tricia had to do to take that first magnificent unaided step on this history-making occasion, was to shift her weight from her back foot to her front foot, lift the back foot off the floor and set it in front of the front foot. Simple procedure. Everything was in readiness and little Tricia Ann stood alone and began the process. Suppose somehow she pushed off too hard with the back foot and shifted her weight too far forward. Not having the strength in her muscles to hold that kind of balance, she would fall on the floor and push her nose into the carpet. What would Dad do? He would stand up, flip off the lights, cut the camera and tape recorder, pick her up by the seat of her diapers and dump her in the crib. He would brush his hands together in a gesture of finality and say, "That's it, kid. You had your chance to learn to walk."

Is that how it happens? Of course not. Tricia Ann continues to try to walk until she walks.

How long do we continue to learn our business or profession? Until we've learned it. How long do we continue to work toward a goal? Until we reach it.

If there is one quality that is possessed by the achievers of the world it is persistence. To get through the hardest journey we need take only one step at a time, but we must keep on stepping. Roger Bannister, the first man to run the mile in less than four minutes, knew the power of persistence. In a time when no one believed man was physically capable of breaking the four minute barrier, Bannister began a training program to accomplish it. In a TV interview several years ago he revealed that the regimen included running, six hours a day, every day, for *eight years*.

People of greatness have climbed the ladder to success while encountering all of the obstacles Mr. Defeated has had, and many times even more. At the bottom of that ladder sit those tragic souls who populate the gutters of the world.

Every person is given situations in life which either conquer him—or he conquers them. One fellow, living in one of the concrete caves formed by the bridges which pass over the freeways of Los Angeles, told a reporter that he was robbed of his one thousand dollars in savings and had no place to go, so he chose to live under freeways. This growing tribe of sub-freeway people call themselves "the Troll Family," after the mysterious, cranky creatures of Scandinavian legend who haunted out-of-the-way places. People choose to live that way!

Given the same situation, Mr. Success will persist in looking for a job, searching for an opportunity, and climbing up from his circumstances.

Between Mr. Defeated and Mr. Success is that vast population of Mediocre. They never quite make their goals or realize their dreams; they can explain their mediocrity in very credible terms: "I didn't have enough education." "My wife (or my husband) didn't help me." "I'm too old." "I've just had a lot of bad breaks." "I'm too young." "But I have a physical disability." "I don't have enough money." "It's because of my racial background."

George Bernard Shaw had his first five novels rejected. Richard Wagner considered the first thirty years of his life a failure; his first opera was so bad he couldn't finish it. His second opera was so bad no one would produce it. His third opera opened and closed the same night. He owed money all over Europe and frequently had to sneak out of town to avoid debtors' prison.

The persistent man or woman doesn't accept defeat; he just keeps on keeping on. David Schwartz, in his book, *The Magic of Thinking Big*, says, "Salvage something from every setback."

Nature is a mirror of the power of persistence. Consider the small seed as it makes its way toward light and in the process separates and cracks several inches of asphalt. Along the California coast the magnificent cypress trees are bent by the unrelenting forces of nature, and yet their beauty is enhanced by their struggle for survival.

Persistence

Joni Eareckson was a beautiful young girl when a diving accident left her completely paralyzed from the neck down. Through God's strength and an incredible amount of persistence, she taught herself to paint by holding a brush in her teeth. She has written two major best sellers, and she has starred in a motion picture of her own life. She is married and has a world-wide ministry, "Joni and Friends."

Corporal Harvey Martin was hit by a grenade in Vietnam and left a paraplegic. His lifelong dream was to run in the Olympics. However, having useless legs did not stop his desire to compete. He began working out with weights and now throws the discus and javelin, lifts weights and has learned archery. A story about Martin appeared in the November, 1980, issue of *Success*. Since this book is being written some years later, I thought I would try to trace Martin and find out what he is doing now. When he answered the phone he rocked me out of my chair. His voice came across with a big smile and his conversation was peppered with positiveness. To keep himself out in the world, he participates in exhibition basketball games during school assemblies. "I tell the kids that my wheel chair is not a burden, only a bad attitude is."

His dream of the Olympics? "Oh, I'm going into training again. I just missed qualifying for the 1980 Para-Olympics, but I'm not going to give up."

How Long Will You Keep On?

In the decade of the 1950s a father in Wheaton, Illinois, was reading the Bible to his children. They were squirming, yawning, and bored, as children will be when they don't want to hear something they don't understand. Ken Taylor had ten children, so that was a pretty big group to keep interested. Suddenly, an idea hit him. Why not take the Bible and translate its thoughts, instead of doing a word-for-word translation from the original Greek and Hebrew? He wrote out a few verses in this way, and from that beginning came the best selling book of all time.

For six years, riding a commuter train to Chicago, Taylor worked on converting parts of the New Testament into a biblical translation that everyone could understand. Finally he took his bulky manuscript to a publisher, who turned it down. The second and third publisher rejected it, too, saying that "No one would be interested." He took his savings and published it himself, but at the end of a year only 800 copies had been sold.

However, with persistence in the face of many discouraging odds, Taylor continued to paraphrase the entire New Testament, and eventually, the entire Bible. Today *The Living Bible* has sold over 25,000,000 copies and has been translated into more than 100 languages. All this because of a father's love for his children, and his persistence toward achieving his goal.

Persistence can turn adversity into greatness. Although the following story has been repeated many times, I believe it is the one I remember the most. This man lost his job in 1832. He was defeated for the legislature, also in 1832. He failed in business in 1833. He was elected to the legislature in 1834. His sweetheart died in 1835. He suffered a nervous breakdown in 1836. He was defeated for Speaker of the House in 1838. He was defeated for nomination for Congress in 1843. He was elected to Congress in 1846. He lost his renomination for Congress in 1848. He was rejected for land officer in 1849. He was defeated for the Senate in 1854. He was defeated for the nomination for vice president of the United States in 1856. He was again defeated for the Senate in 1858. But Abraham Lincoln was elected President of the United States in 1860.

Every time I hear of Lincoln I am reminded to keep on.

Two boys went to start a fire in the school stove one day. Having laid the fire well, they poured kerosene on it to help it start, not knowing that the janitor had mistakenly placed gasoline in the can instead. When the match was struck, a terrible explosion shook the building. One boy was dead and the other was severely injured. The doctor informed the saddened parents they would have to amputate the boy's legs. "Could we wait one day?" pleaded the mother. The doctors agreed. A day at a time they held off the operation, until a month or more had gone by. When the bandages were removed, the right leg was two and one-half inches shorter than the other and the toes of the left foot had been burned almost completely away. But this boy was determined to run. Painstakingly over weeks, months, and years he persisted—from crutches to walking to running. The man, Glenn Cunningham, earned the title "Fastest Human Being." He won Olympic gold medals and was named Athlete of the Century at Madison Square Garden because of his persistence which turned adversity into greatness.

One of my favorite characters in history is Winston Churchill. Twice he took a nation through grave times, twice he served as Prime Minister of Great Britain. He was a man of brilliant powers of communication, an inspiration to millions of people around the world to continue to press on. When he was invited to speak at the commencement exercise at Oxford University, he arrived with his usual accouterments, the big cigar and cane, walked to the platform as people stood and cheered. With the unmatched dignity of the British, he bid them be seated, took off his top hat, laid it on the lectern, and began his address. Looking over that intent audience, he began: "Never give up." For thirty seconds there was silence in that auditorium as the great elder statesman allowed the impact of those few simple words to sink into the hearts and minds of the people to whom he was speaking. Then he repeated: "Never give up." This time he waited a full minute and a half. He looked into the eyes of each one to make sure the full importance of those words was communicated before he continued. "Never give up," he thundered. Then he reached down, picked up his hat, put it on, steadied himself with his cane, and left the platform. His address was finished. That was perhaps the shortest address he had ever delivered in his life, and yet it was one of the most eloquent. Those words echo down through the years to you and to me today.

Recently, at the close of one of my seminars, a lady came to substantiate Churchill's commitment to persistence. She had worked for the great statesman at the close of World War II. One day he came to her and said, "Young woman, you've got a good head on your shoulders. Whatever you set out to do, give it all that is necessary to see it through." A great man committed to a great principle.

Ladder to Your Dreams

Jesse Owens, another man who has been called the fastest human being alive, grew up in Cleveland in a family that he described as "materially poor, but spiritually rich." One day a well-known athlete came to Jesse's school to speak to the students. His name was Charlie Paddock and at one time sportswriters said *he* was the fastest human being alive. Charlie talked to the kids and said, "What do you want to be? You name it and then believe that God will help you get it." Young Jesse looked at Charlie Paddock and thought, *I want to be what Mr. Paddock has been.*

After the speech was over, Jesse went to the sports coach, inspired by his hero, Paddock, and said, "Coach, I've got a dream!"

The coach looked down at this skinny little black boy and said, "What's your dream, son?"

"I want to follow Mr. Paddock as the fastest human being alive."

"It's great to have a dream, Jesse, but to attain your dream you must build a ladder to it." Then he explained: "The first rung is determination! (Persistence!) The second rung is dedication! The third rung is discipline! And the fourth rung is attitude!"

Jesse Owens put his foot on that first rung, that first mental decision to never give up. Determination, persistence, in the face of many challenges. He was the fastest man to ever run the 100-meter dash, the fastest to run the 200-meter. He won four gold medals in the Olympic Games and his name was included in the charter list to be inscribed in the American Hall of Athletic Fame.

All because Jesse had a dream and was willing to climb the ladder to success.

Release the Power within You

One of the energy drains in life is the process of debating, "Will I or won't I?" "Can I or can't I?" "Should I or shouldn't I?" Why not start immediately to say, "I will until"? When you know from the outset "I will do it," then you can concentrate all your time, energy, and talents on doing it now, instead of joining the great debate team with yourself.

A person with persistence will succeed over the person with more talent, more education, or more money.

"Nothing in the world can take the place of persistence. Talent will not. Nothing is more common than unsuccessful men with talent. Genius will not. Unrewarded genius is almost a proverb.

Education will not. The world is full of educated derelicts. Persistence, determination and hard work make the difference" *Calvin Coolidge*.

Lack of persistence is one of the major causes of failure, and yet it is evident that it is a weakness which permeates the human race. In our business, for instance, we see people who charge into the scene with enthusiasm to attain great heights. However, with the first temporary discouragement, they are knocked down one rung on that ladder of their dreams. With the second setback they drop further down, and the third time they're flat on the ground.

A temporary setback is not a total knockout. There is nothing wrong or disgraceful about getting knocked down. Virtually all the greats have experienced temporary defeats. Those are the learning times, the opportunities for you to grow and achieve your destiny. If you get up one more time than you fall, you will make it through.

"Far better it is to dare mighty things, to win glorious triumph even though checked with failure, than to take rank with those poor spirits who neither enjoy much nor suffer much, because they live in the gray twilight that knows not victory nor defeat" *Theodore Roosevelt*.

Only quitting spells defeat.

DON'T QUIT

When things go wrong, as they sometimes will,
When the road you're trudging seems all up hill,
When the funds are low and the debts are high,
And you want to smile, but you have to sigh,
When care is pressing you down a bit,
Rest, if you must—but don't you quit.

Life is queer with its twists and turns,
As everyone of us sometimes learns,
And many a failure turns about
When he might have won had he stuck it out;
Don't give up, though the pace seems slow—
You might succeed with another blow.

Often the goal is nearer than

It seems to a faint and faltering man,
Often the struggler has given up
When he might have captured the victor's cup.
And he learned too late, when the night slipped down,
How close he was to the golden crown.

Success is failure turned inside out—
The silver tint of the clouds of doubt—
And you never can tell how close you are,
It may be near when it seems afar;
So stick to the fight when you're hardest hit—
It's when things seem worst that you mustn't quit.*

*From *Lines to Live By,* Thomas Nelson, Inc., Clinton Howell, 1972, p. 178.

14

THE GREAT
MULTIPLYING FACTOR

My Dynamic Living Seminar was over and I was leaving the auditorium when a young man approached me with a question that so many ask: "Look, I can see that there are certain principles that bring success in life . . . and I can accept that all of us have tremendous abilities. Isn't that enough? If I have these capabilities within me somewhere and I can learn the principles, does it really make any major difference what my self-image is?"

My response to him that Saturday afternoon, and to everyone who might ask that question, is: IT MAKES ALL THE DIFFERENCE IN THE WORLD!

You may be the most talented person who ever lived; you may know the principles of success backwards and forward; you may have listened to hours of tapes and read every book available on the subject of human motivation, success, and failure. However, you may not be achieving even a small portion of your potential.

Positive thinking does not always work, particularly when it is in direct contrast with the picture you have of yourself.

Your self-image is the sum total of attitudes, facts, and feelings which you have accumulated about yourself. Everything that we think, feel, and do is experienced in such a way to be consistent with the picture which has been developed on the inside. Consequently, you may be a very gifted singer, possess the ability to entertain others, but if you do not believe that about yourself, you will never use that ability to its full potential.

Joyce Brothers, well-known author, columnist, and psychologist, described it this way: "An individual's self-concept is the core of his personality. It affects every aspect of human behavior: the ability to learn, the capacity to grow and change, the choice of friends, mates, and careers. It's no exaggeration to say that a strong positive self-image is the best possible preparation for success in life."

Who *do* you think you are? The final ingredient in the Magic Formula for Dynamic Living is the multiplying power of a proper self-image. Since none of us have reached our full potential in life, we must talk about changing the self-image from what it is today to what we would like it to be. Is that possible? Can the image be changed? Are you "locked in" to the patterns of thought already developed, or can you become a different type of person?

The great news I have to share with you in this final chapter is that you *can* change. You can become any kind of person you choose to be.

That change is a process—an ongoing, exhilarating journey. It can be started with five basic steps.

One: Understand the Source of Your Self-Image

The image you have of yourself today exists because of the experiences of the past. Those experiences have not made you the way you are, they have made you *believe* you are the way you are. Some people have taught that we are a product of our environment. After all, it was reasoned, you can't blame a kid for antisocial behavior when he came from a bad background. However, few people believe that today, because we can look at two kids from the same environment, the same parents and surroundings, and one becomes a professional athlete or successful business person, while the other ends up in the penitentiary. Environment has not made you the way you are; experiences of the past have not made you the way you are. However, they did begin to form powerful patterns of thought in your subconscious mind, habitual ways of thinking about yourself, that continue to affect your whole experience of life.

The first identity crisis in your life occurred the day you were born. For 250 days, more or less, you were blissfully comfortable in a cozy apartment where your needs were met. Perhaps once in a while there were some unpleasant experiences that disturbed your tranquility, but, in general, you were warm and well-fed, secure in your little nest. However, through no fault of your own, you lost your lease! You were forcefully evicted from your first home . . . someone grabbed you by the ankles, whacked you across the backside and said, "Welcome to the world!"

"Wait a minute, it's cold out here," you thought, and started to cry about the trauma which was inflicted upon you.

You don't remember that day, but from that time on, the experiences you have had began to have an effect upon who you think you are. Very early in life you may have known that you were loved and appreciated, and you began to thrive; or you may have been deprived of that initial cuddling and caring which is so vital to healthy growth.

I believe, as many doctors do, that your self-image began to be formed early in life. In fact, there are some who believe that image was in the development stage even before you were born. It seems reasonable to believe that any negative emotion within the human body will develop a negative chemistry; conversely, any positive emotion will develop a positive chemistry. During the time you were carried in your mother's womb, there were occasions when she underwent great stress, anger, jealousy, or worry, which are all negative emotions. That negative chemistry began to have an affect upon who you think you are. But wait a minute! Before you blame your mother for your difficulties because of her emotional upsets when she was pregnant, let me add that negative chemistry in the womb, the traumatic birth process, and those beginning relationships with mom and dad, siblings and friends, did not make you the way you are. However, they did begin to have an affect upon who you *think* you are. Those early circumstances and the way in which you reacted to them began developing a picture.

What a shame that many people believe those pictures are irreversible and do nothing about the way they are; in fact, they are the ones who say, "Well, that's just the way I am. I can't really help it."

For example, consider the girl who was always late to work. Morning after morning, she walked in ten or fifteen minutes late. She was asked, "Doesn't it bother you to be late to work every morning?"

"Oh, not really," she replied indifferently.

"Aren't you afraid you may lose your job because of your tardiness?"

She shrugged her shoulders, "It's just the way I am, there's nothing I can do about it."

Somehow she had programmed herself into thinking that she couldn't be on time. She was wrong. We are not locked into any image of the past. We have been made to believe we are the way we are because of past programming.

As a youngster I wanted to be like my dad. Please understand that my dad was never mechanically inclined, and Mother often reinforced that belief by saying, "Leave it alone, dear, I'll call the plumber." He never did anything mechanical around the house; consequently, I began to develop the impression that I was not so inclined, either. The aptitude tests I took all through school verified my belief, since the lowest scores I received were in, of course, mechanical aptitude. My school counselors confirmed this view: "Don't try to do anything that has to do with technical or mechanical abilities, Skip, you're bound to fail. You'd better deal with people."

I developed a picture of myself as a mechanical clod.

Another image of my past pertained to dancing. I was raised in a conservative Christian home and was taught that it was wrong to dance. When I went to school it was not socially acceptable for me to say, "Sorry, I don't want to dance with you sinners." The comfortable escape was to mumble, "Sorry, I don't know how to dance. I'm not graceful, I'm really clumsy and uncoordinated. I just can't dance, you see." I knew all of the excuses. For years I got out of dancing at school with that story.

Those impressions of myself were parts of my self-image that developed as a result of ideas communicated to me by the authority figures in my life, and my limited, childish understanding of "my world."

What opinions do you have of yourself that were nurtured by the important people in your life? Some of you may have been led to believe that "things" are more important than you are. What happens to children, for instance? Imagine the time you cut the corner too close while walking around a table, and knocked a vase to the ground. Perhaps this wasn't an ordinary glass jar, but a family solid crystal heirloom. You were in for a whale of a licking, isolation in your room, and a few angry words thrown in for good measure. Because you could not logically reason at this point, you felt, "Boy, I guess a vase is more important than I am."

In the process of rearing children, even the best parents have had the occasion to imply to their offspring that objects, "things," have more value than people.

By the time you and I reached the age of two, 50 percent of what we ever believed about ourselves had been formed; by the age of six, 60 percent of our self-belief had been established, and by the age of eight, about 80 percent. By the time we reached the age of fourteen, over 99 percent of us had a well-developed sense of inferiority.

Unless you have taken some time in your life to change your image, you may still be walking around today with an inferiority complex.

"I'm getting along pretty well," you may tell me. "I don't have a complex and I'm not inferior!" Many of us find ways to cope with an inferiority complex; for instance, we compensate. I discovered early in life that the best way to counteract some of the inferiority I felt was to try to become intellectually superior because I believed I was less than average in everything else. I found acceptance by striving for high grades.

Some people find the way to handle those feelings is to become superior physically. When I went to school, we called those kids "bullies." Inside they may feel small, so outside they push everyone around. Other ways of wrestling with those low esteem feelings are to become inconspicuous, quiet, or shy. Some try to handle them by becoming talkative, chattering all the time. We have a variety of ways to cope.

The first step to changing a self-image is to understand its source. Where did all those feelings originate? What was the input in the early part of life?

Think of it! A majority of the image is formed before one can reason or communicate. That means that most of it is formed by emotional response and incomplete, immature understanding and perception. This becomes a critically important point in the second step of our process.

Second Step: Believe Your Self-Image Can Be Changed

"You can't teach an old dog new tricks." That's a falsehood. A vast majority of people believe they are locked into the kind of person they are and there's nothing they can do about it.

At one point in my life I could have given you a personality description of myself which I thought was accurate. "I am quiet, shy, and backward. I don't like talking to people. I don't like being in front of people because I'm just a very average guy." I couldn't do anything above average, and if anything ever happened that gave me recognition, I had an explanation. For instance, when I was in college I was elected student body president. However, I believed it wasn't because they really wanted me, but the result of three kids in my class who knew everybody on campus and talked them into voting for me. That's the way I explained that honor to myself.

Some of you are still walking around with attitudes about yourself that you shouldn't have. I came to that point in my life when I began to believe that I could change. If many of those thought patterns about me were incorrect in their origin, then the errors could be corrected.

One day I was at my brother's home when his fourteen-year-old son came running into the living room where we were chatting, and said, "Dad, the lawn mower won't work." That was not a teen-age ruse. David, my nephew, really wanted to mow the lawn.

By this time I had begun to believe that I could change my image and behavior, and I said, "David, let me take a look at it."

You should have seen the expression on his face! Uncle Skip, the mechanically inept, went out to the garage and started to fool with the lawn mower. I took a screw driver and some pliers and began to pull things apart; before I knew it, I had the whole engine spread out on the floor. I cleaned some dirty parts, messed around with this and that, made several adjustments, and then faced the challenge of putting it back together. I had never done that before. Soon I had all the pieces where I thought they went, and the moment of truth arrived. I reached down, grabbed the pull cord, and the lawn mower sprang into action. Boy, was I excited! I mowed the whole lawn with David cheering me onward.

You may think that is a silly thing, but I discovered that day I could do things I never believed possible before in my life.

The picture I had developed of not having mechanical aptitude had nothing to do with my ability; it revolved around a childish perception of what it meant to be like my father.

Remember the guy with the two left feet who insisted he couldn't dance? At one time I was a member of a singing group called the Sanborn Singers. I was comfortable with that, because God had given me a singing voice, and I knew that was one thing I could do. However, we had a dramatic musical production scheduled and a wiry little choreographer was hired to teach us to dance. This man had been in show business all his life, was very agile and coordinated . . . the kind of a guy who could stand up straight, bend over, and put his forehead on his shins.

The first day of rehearsal, I said, "Look, Alex, there's something you have to understand about me. I was raised in a minister's home, and I've never danced in my life. I am not coordinated, I'm clumsy. So when you put the show together, if you could just put me in the singing parts, I'd sure appreciate it, because I can't dance."

Those words hit me with tremendous force! It was then I realized that if I were going to continue teaching a seminar in which I told people that they could do anything they set their mind to do, I was going to have to learn how to dance!

Well, I was the most uncoordinated guy you have ever seen when I began. But one day I went into one of the rehearsal rooms where they had mirrors around the walls and ballet bars. I grabbed hold of the bar and looked in that mirror and said, "Feet, you have something to learn and I'm going to teach you." I started with step, brush-brush, step-step, and repeated it over and over again.

In the next year I traveled with the show and danced for over two hundred thousand people.

You can change! But you must believe that you can become a different type of person!

Third Step: Decide What Kind of a Person
You Would Like to Be

If you could be any kind of a person in the world, what would you like to be? I did not ask, "Who would you like to be?" You are you! I am not asking you to become someone else, I am challenging you to become the best "You" that is possible. That's enough. What kind of person would you be if you were the BEST YOU?

Most people don't know the answer to the previous question. They have never taken the time and energy to figure out the traits and characteristics they would like to possess. I believe there are three ways you can decide the kind of person you want to be. The first one is for all of us; the second one is for those who believe in Scripture; the third one is for those of you who do not believe in Scripture.

First, you meet people every day of your life, and you probably see a characteristic in them that you like. It flashes through your mind, "I wish I were like that." Whenever you see a quality in someone that you like, that would be true of you, appropriate that virtue and decide that is the way you are. Shakespeare said, "Assume a virtue and it's yours." We meet people from day to day and are impressed by certain things about them. If they are worthwhile, take those qualities as your own. "That's just the way I am."

For those of you who believe in Scripture, look at the life of

Jesus. Write a full character description of the kind of person he was and then begin to appropriate those traits for yourself. Become that kind of a person.

If you don't believe in Scripture, look at the lives of great men and women down through the centuries, and discover what it was about them that made them great. What characteristic would you pick of Abraham Lincoln? Honesty. Pierre and Madame Curie? Persistence. Will Rogers? Humor. Mother Teresa? Compassion. Winston Churchill? Wisdom.

With these three methods, you should be able to begin to develop a new picture of the kind of person you want to be.

Fourth Step: Write It Down

Have you heard this one before? It is an amazing thing to me how many people can hear these principles, read them, and nod in agreement, and then neglect to write down who it is they want to be as a person. Frequently people have said, "Skip, it's just not working like I thought it would," or some similar discouraging statement. The first question I ask most people is, "Have you taken the time to write down the kind of person you want to be?" Most of the time the answer is an embarrassed, "Not really." That's vital to the whole picture and, I believe, the most important part of the entire dynamic living formula.

Take a book, a sheet of paper, or file cards and write a personal description of the kind of person you want to be. These statements should be made in the present, positive tense, not "I hope to be," or "I want to be," or "I will be." That is future terminology where tomorrow never comes. Make the statements in the present, positive state—"I am," "I have," "I do." Will they be statements of reality? Not yet. But it is a positive statement of faith.

Decide who you want to be. That is far more important than the material things you want, or your achievements in business or professional endeavors. If you don't decide what kind of a person you want to be, you may come to a point in your life where the things you thought you wanted don't fit together with the person you have become.

It is important to write it down. I have a little notebook that I carry around which is worn with age and use. In spite of its shabby appearance it is very special to me, because it contains pages of who I am as a person. I'm not the same person I was ten years ago, or even two years ago. I will be a different person two years from now because that's the way I plan it. I'm not talking about some wild ego-trip. This book was not written to try and impress you with my greatness. It is written to challenge you to become all *you* were created to be.

There is no such thing in life as status quo. You do not remain where you are; you are either in the process of improving and growing, or you are in the process of decaying and dying. The choice is yours.

One man wrote that he had been diagnosed as a schizophrenic. His life was filled with fear and anxiety. Then he wrote out a description of the self-image he wanted to have, and read it every day. People started to ask him about his improved confidence and enthusiasm, and soon better job opportunities came to him. He began to reach his goals of owning a restaurant and teaching other people to say yes to their potential.

Another man shared with me that he had written down the image he wanted. He began to apply all of the principles, and for the next six months after he started this process, this is what happened: his very expensive purebred dog ran away; he lost his lucrative job; his fiancée left him; he was forced to leave his home, because he couldn't afford the payments. This doesn't sound like very positive results, does it? However, this is what he said: "Throughout this six-month period I read my goals daily on what I wanted to accomplish. I read the Bible every day, trying, I believe now, to find something to contradict what you had said so that I could quit all this stuff."

He continued to describe the next year, in which he started a new business that flourished, he moved back into his own home, he met another girl who supported his dreams and goals. Within two years he had eighteen full-time and part-time employees.

It is your responsibility to be the kind of person you choose to be. You can no longer say, "Well, if my husband (or wife) were

just a little bit better, I'd be." Or, "If it weren't for my background, I would be better off." It's not their fault. It's yours. This
was tough for me to face, and is probably tough for you.

Fifth Step: Spend Time with the Person You Want to Be

People have said to me, "Skip, I can't be around those people I
want to be like all the time. Churchill, Lincoln, Will Rogers aren't
available to me." I understand that, but remember, we are not
striving to become a clone of someone else, we are moving toward
becoming the best kind of person we choose to be.

Spending time with the person you want to be is the process of
reading that profile you've written about yourself, every day. I
believe it ought to be done every morning and every night, out loud
to yourself in the mirror, whenever possible.

I don't know what statements you will make about yourself. But
let me give you a couple of examples so you may begin to understand what I'm thinking about in this regard.

"I am the kind of person who faces every adversity of life with
the attitude that the seeds of a greater benefit will emerge."

"I am the kind of person who accepts criticism without
resentment."

Most people are not like those statements; I have not always
been that way, either. But I was inspired to make the latter statement of faith after a friend shared this story with me. He travels
around the country speaking for seminars. One week-end he was
invited to speak to a group of ministers and their wives. When he
arrived at the meeting he was told, "By the way, there are many of
these ministers who do not believe that the Bible is the inspired
word of God."

My friend looked at them and said, "Why didn't you tell me
that before I came?"

"Well, we were afraid you wouldn't have come if you had
known," was the sheepish reply.

"You're probably right, but I'm here and we're going to have a
good time."

When he began to speak he decided he was going to quote every

Scripture to them that he could remember. This was a man who had spent years reading and studying the Scriptures. He told me, "I started to quote, and I quoted Scripture for two hours; when it was over I dismissed in prayer, left the auditorium, and went straight to my room. The next day, when the morning session began, I said, "Let's talk a bit about what you felt about my talk last night."

The pastor of a very large, liberal church stood up and said, "That was the most ridiculous bit of illogical thinking. It didn't make sense, and I thought it was the worst presentation I've ever heard." This Doctor of Divinity continued for about fifteen minutes with the most scathing criticism. It was an intellectual hatchet job.

When he sat down, my friend looked at him and said, "Sir, I thank you. That was a marvelous statement. Do all of you understand how beautiful this is and what happened here? In just the two short hours we were together last night, this man was able to develop a sense of relationship that allowed him to make those remarks to me. I want you to know, sir, that I am comfortable for you to feel that way. Does anyone else have something to say?"

For the next few minutes another man with a Ph.D. after his name proceeded to rip him up one side and down the other. He threw my friend on the ground verbally. "This is amazing," my friend replied. "In such a short time two of you were able to develop that rapport which allowed you to be able to disagree so strongly. That's exciting! Would anyone else like to say something?"

At the close of that weekend conference, both of those men came to him at separate times and said, "This has been the most meaningful weekend I have ever attended. I just wanted to say 'thank you.'"

Why the attitude change? Because they found somebody who knew where he was going. He was so confident in what he believed that he didn't have to return the attack or justify his statements. He was not in the process of comparing himself with other people; he had decided who he was.

It's a positive experience in life to have someone cut you apart with criticism and not feel resentment or the need for revenge or justification.

Write down the kind of person you really want to be and invest enough time with the description and those characteristics that you begin to become like that person.

My actions are not always what my intentions are, but my behavior comes closer to my intentions the longer I live with the person I have chosen to be.

The more time we spend with people, the more we become like them. I am told that over a period of years, husband and wife not only start to act and talk in similar fashion, they even begin to look like one another. Those years of close association develop many similarities. As we continue to live with our own image, we become more firmly entrenched in that image, even to the point that it begins to show on our countenance.

I have a friend who does makeup work at the Metropolitan Opera in Boston. He said, "Skip, you know I've made up thousands and thousands of faces over forty-five years of working in the makeup industry in the opera. I've discovered an interesting thing: What you talk about in your seminars is very true. The lines of a person's face begin to reflect the kind of experience of life one is living. If people are negatively oriented toward life, over a period of years they will begin to form the lines of a frown. They don't know it, but they can be frowning without realizing it. It works the other way, too. The happy, excited, positively oriented people ultimately form the lines of a smile."

The story is told that an aide came to Abraham Lincoln and said, "There's a man outside who is waiting to see you about a job in government." Lincoln is reported to have said, "I am not interested in talking with him." His aide said, "But you haven't looked at his resumé, sir, you don't know anything about him."

Lincoln replied, "I'm sorry, but I don't need to talk with him. I saw his face and believe that by the time a man reaches his age he is responsible for the look on his face, and I don't like his expression."

The lines of your face tend to reflect your experience of life. They tend to mirror the kind of person you have chosen to be. You are responsible for the kind of life you live, for the image you have of yourself. But the good news is, you are not locked into any image of the past. You can change and be the best *you* that you were created to be.

You are unique, one of a kind. No one else can fill the particular place in the world in which you live. You are endowed with talents great or small that are priceless when used to their fullest. You can be considerate, kind, and sympathetic, or a proverbial pain in the neck. You can grumble, gripe, and complain that you never had a chance, or you can go out tomorrow and do your job better than it was done today and create your own opportunities.

You can fill your mind with the world's finest thoughts or pick up a trashy novel and pore over it in some secret place.

You will leave this earth someday a bit better or a bit worse for your living. You must accept the responsibility that is inherent in your greatness.

This entire book was meant to be a challenge.

The Challenge

I want to challenge you with who you are and who you can be.

The challenge is to recognize and grasp your God-given equipment; to utilize those universal principles which will move your life forward in an exciting experience if you will learn and apply them. I challenge you to become a better person, to write down the kind of person you want to be and invest time with that person every day.

If you will do those things, your life will change for the better, you will learn to live dynamically and experience a life that is filled with joy and happiness, free of fear and free of worry, continually in the process of accomplishing worthwhile goals.

It is important to gain balance in those six major areas of life which include your business, your home, your social, your physical, your mental, and your spiritual life. Then you will understand what life was designed to be: an exciting, exhilarating experience! You'll find that you will be able to get up every morning and say, "It's a marvelous day to be alive!"

If you have read this far and have not concluded that the only way to reach your full potential is with a balanced spiritual life, then now is the time to consider that Jesus Christ is the author of all joy, happiness, peace, and strength. He said, "I came that they might have life, and that they might have it abundantly" (John 10:10, KJV). He keeps his promises, to be with us always, if we accept him as our Lord and Savior.

As a boy of ten, I made the decision to accept Christ into my life. And every day I live I see more and more wisdom in that decision.

Have you invited him into your life? I invite you to do that now!

My friends, SAY YES TO YOUR POTENTIAL!

AFTERWORD

Does it work? The first time I heard Skip Ross in a Dynamic Living Seminar I was skeptical. The type of life he described seemed far from reality. In a world where tragedy, disappointments, and disillusionment is more the norm than the exception, I thought his formula was simplistic and unattainable.

However, as I cautiously began to apply the formula to my own life, I began to experience the "magic." Our son, who was sixteen years old when he first heard Skip, gained new feelings of self-worth as a result of the formula. My husband, who traveled for a year with Skip in a pageant called "The Great American Dream," observed the daily examples of principles of success in action. Our daughter typed this manuscript and interrupted her work to run to the telephone, call a friend, and say, "This is exciting . . . let me read you something!"

This book was born when I approached Skip and said, "Your material is too good to stay within the walls of an auditorium. Why don't we write a book?" I visited Circle A Ranch in Rockford, Michigan, which is the result of one of Skip and Susan's dreams, a beautiful place where young people learn these principles that are never taught in school, but are the most vital elements in leading a happy, productive life. I've read hundreds of letters from people who have said that their lives have been changed from the seminars and tapes. Most of these letters could not be printed, because Skip Ross is not on an ego trip to edify himself, and the accolades would be embarrassing.

My original skepticism turned to belief as I saw the power of God work through a man who climbed up from the bottom to help thousands live happier, more fulfilling lives. The source material for this book is the best in the world, which is the reason the Magic Formula for Dynamic Living works. Try it. I did, and I love it.

CAROLE C. CARLSON

BIBLIOGRAPHY

Bland, Glenn. *Success*. Wheaton, Ill.: Tyndale House Publishers, 1981.

Conn, Paul. *Making It Happen*. Old Tappan, N.J.: Fleming H. Revell, 1981.

Dobson, Dr. James. *Dare to Discipline*. Wheaton, Ill.: Tyndale House Publishers, 1973.

Howell, Clinton T. *Lines to Live By*. Nashville: Thomas Nelson, 1972.

Jones, Charlie. *Life is Tremendous*. Wheaton, Ill.: Tyndale House Publishers, 1968.

Keller, Helen. *The Faith of Helen Keller*. Kansas City: Hallmark Cards, 1967.

Key, Wilson Bryan. *Subliminal Seduction*. Englewood Cliffs, N.J.: Prentice Hall, 1974.

————. *Media Sexploitation*, Englewood Cliffs, N.J.: Prentice Hall, 1976.

Marshall, Eric and Hample, Stuart. *Children's Letters to God*. New York: Simon & Schuster, 1966.

Moruzzi, Dr. G. and Magoun, Dr. H. W. *The Waking Brain*, Springfield, Ill.: Charles C. Thomas, 1969.

Neuman, James. *Release Your Brakes*, New York: Warner Books, 1978.

Peale, Norman Vincent. *Creative Help for Daily Living*. Pawling, N.Y.: Foundation for Christian Living, 1979.

Penfield, Dr. Wilder. *Speech and Brain Mechanisms*. Princeton, N.J.: Princeton University Press, 1959.

Schwartz, David. *The Magic of Thinking Big*. Englewood Cliffs, N.J.: Prentice Hall, 1959.

Shinn, George. *The Miracle of Motivation*. Wheaton, Ill.: Tyndale House Publishers, 1981.

Stoop, Dr. David. *Self Talk*. Old Tappan, N.J.: Fleming H. Revell, 1982.

Thomas, Paul. *Psychofeedback*. Englewood Cliffs, N.J.: Prentice Hall, 1977.

Wynn, J. S. *How Christian Parents Face Family Problems*, Philadelphia: Westminster Press, 1955.

Ziglar, Zig. *See You at the Top*, Gretna, La.: Pelican Publishing Co., 1982.